# HALVERG.
# &
# TUNSTALL
# REMEMBERED

## LIMITED EDITION

## Sheila Hutchinson

*Sheila Hutchinson*

Front Cover Photograph: Halvergate Corn Mill in working order in the 1920s.Photograph supplied by Peter Allard.

Back Cover Photograph: The Village Sign photographed in 2013. This sign was unveiled in 1978 by Amy Youngs.

ISBN 9780957462311


Published
by
Sheila & Paul Hutchinson
7, Colman Avenue,
Stoke Holy Cross,
Norwich,
Norfolk.
NR14 8NA
e-mail address:
paul.sheila844@btinternet.com


Printed
by
Really Useful Print Co. Ltd.
Bessemer Rd.
Norwich.

## PREFACE

I have written this book about Halvergate as, on doing my family tree research, I found that lots of my ancestors' relations, mainly the Hewitt family, lived at Halvergate and the surrounding areas. This gave me an interest in the area.
King Billy Hewitt from Berney Arms would often take his horse to be shod at the blacksmith in Halvergate village and would meet up with his friends at the Red Lion and they would all have a drink together.

Halvergate was and still is a pleasant and attractive village and is now a conservation area with many listed buildings.


## INTRODUCTION

The parishes of Halvergate and Tunstall have a long history and were well established by the time of the Norman Conquest, and both are mentioned in the Domesday Book of 1086.

The earliest evidence of human activity in the parish comes in the form of prehistoric flint flakes. The next evidence comes from a few Neolithic finds, a flint axe-head and some pottery fragments.

Aerial photographs show circular crop-marks which are believed to be evidence of structures from the Bronze Age. Other crop-marks are visible which are thought to be evidence of early Roman occupation of the area. There has been many finds over the years of pottery fragments and coins as well as other items such as brooches and armlets etc. from the Roman period indicating that there may have buildings around the villages at that time.

During the Roman period all of the current marshland of these parishes was under a Great Estuary and only the Halvergate and Tunstall villages themselves were above sea level. They would have been coastal villages around that time.

There is evidence of salt pans in the area where the evaporation of seawater to produce salt was carried out providing further evidence of occupation around that period.

The marshes cover the major area of the Halvergate and Tunstall parishes and, probably, for several hundreds of years have been drained in order that the land could be used. Drainage was probably achieved in the early days by man made and natural drainage channels, but over the last about 300 years by wind pumps and then more recently by steam pumps and electric pumps.

## HALVERGATE PARISH POPULATION FROM CENSUS RETURNS.

| YEAR | POPULATION | MALE | FEMALE | HOUSES |
|------|-----------|------|--------|--------|
| 1801 | 397 | 207 | 190 | 59 |
| 1811 | 392 | 191 | 201 | 79 |
| 1821 | 449 | 217 | 232 | 76 |
| 1831 | 465 | 227 | 238 | 84 |
| 1841 | 495 | 253 | 242 | 104 |
| 1851 | 545 | 296 | 249 | 117 |
| 1861 | 541 | 267 | 274 | 117 |
| 1871 | 452 | | | 115 |
| 1881 | 482 | 237 | 245 | 129 |
| 1891 | 504 | 238 | 266 | 118 |
| 1901 | 455 | 229 | 226 | 110 |
| 1911 | 473 | 236 | 237 | 109 |
| 1921 | 419 | 199 | 220 | 106 |
| 1931 | 419 | 215 | 204 | 118 |
| 1951 | 502 | 258 | 244 | 153 |
| 1961 | 440 | 210 | 230 | 152 |
| 1991 | 439 | | | |

## TUNSTALL PARISH POPULATION FROM CENSUS RETURNS.

| YEAR | POPULATION | MALE | FEMALE | HOUSES |
|------|-----------|------|--------|--------|
| 1801 | 45 | 21 | 24 | |
| 1811 | 74 | 36 | 38 | |
| 1821 | 79 | 43 | 36 | |
| 1831 | 101 | 52 | 49 | 10 |
| 1841 | 116 | 60 | 56 | 20 |
| 1851 | 139 | 75 | 64 | 25 |
| 1861 | 112 | 63 | 49 | 25 |
| 1871 | 117 | | | |
| 1881 | 106 | 50 | 56 | 23 |
| 1891 | 131 | 59 | 72 | 22 |
| 1901 | 107 | 55 | 52 | 21 |
| 1911 | 97 | 54 | 43 | 19 |
| 1921 | 79 | 46 | 33 | 16 |
| 1931 | 94 | 55 | 39 | 22 |

## AREA

### TUNSTALL PARISH
In the year 1831 the area of Tunstall parish was listed as 1,300 acres. From 1851, though to 1931 the area was given as 1,612 acres.

### HALVERGATE PARISH
The area of the parish was quoted in the year 1831 as 2,630 acres, between 1851 and 1881 it was given as 2,675 acres, and from 1891 to 1931 the area was given as 2,712 acres.

Following the Norfolk Review Order of 1935 the enlarged Halvergate parish became 6069 acres.

This was due to the incorporation of:

1,595 acres of Tunstall Parish, which was abolished,

609 acres of the detached marshlands of Acle Parish,

397 acres of South Walsham parish detached marshland.

365 acres of Postwick detached marshland,

222 acres of Cantley detached marshland, and

169 acres of Burlingham St Andrews, which was abolished.

**The sketch map below shows the parish boundaries before and after the 1935 changes.**

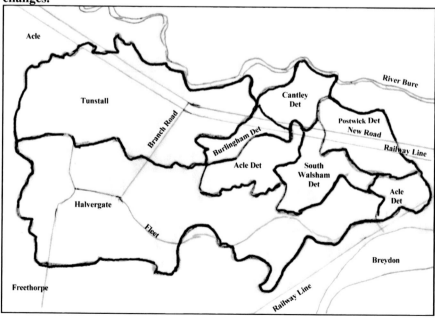

# ACLE NEW ROAD & BRANCH ROAD TURNPIKE TOLL ROADS

The Acle New road cuts through the old Tunstall parish, and connected the Suspension Bridge at Great Yarmouth to Acle. It was built in 1831. Prior to its construction the road to Acle from Great Yarmouth was via Caister and was about 3 and a half miles longer. There was no proper road from Halvergate to Great Yarmouth and the journey would have been across the marsh tracks and along the embankment running alongside the Halvergate Fleet and then alongside the Breydon wall.

## Norfolk Chronicle - 23rd April 1831

*'On Wednesday, the 13th inst. pursuant to advertisement, the Acting Trustees of the new Acle and Yarmouth Turnpike, with John Prentice Esq. their chairman, the Rev. Charles Penrice, H. N. Borroughs Esq. T. H. Batcheler, Esq. R. Cory Esq. C. Nichols Esq. W. W. Branford Esq. and other gentlemen, met at the Suspension Bridge, on the North Quay, to walk over the line of road, and inspect the progress of the works. - It appears that the bridge over Tunstall Boat Dyke is complete; the arches and trunks over Land Spring Drains, the Mill Drains, and the entire line of road formed, and that to complete it, previously to its being opened to the public, the materials (which are broken stones and shingles) remain to be laid on, and these are actually prepared, and landed over the river wall, whence they will be conveyed in boats down the dykes to different parts of the roads. - The Trustees were accompanied by Mr. Isaac Lenny, of Norwich, the company's surveyor, by Mr. Thorold, the Contractor, and other gentlemen and the Trustees were pleased to express their gratification at the manner the works were going on, and afterwards an excellent dinner, provided at Acle Queen's Head, in Mr. England's best style. - perhaps it is not generally known, that the saving of distance from Acle to Yarmouth will be three miles and five furlongs, and a great advantage of the project is, that by means of the branches, a large tract of the country will be laid open to Yarmouth, which has hitherto been nearly excluded for a great part of the year, on account of the distance of roads by a very circuitous route. In addition to the satisfaction which the trustees feel at the progress of the works, the shareholders have the gratification of knowing that they will receive ample interest on the principal money, invested so judiciously, and with so much public spirit in this useful undertaking.'*

Tollgates were erected along the Acle New Road, one at the Yarmouth end in Runham detached, one at the Acle - Tunstall parish boundaries and a further tollgate near the Stracey Arms at the junction of Branch Road with the New Road. A further tollgate was erected at the junction of Branch Road with Marsh Road at Wooden Hut Corner in Halvergate.

The Tunstall Tithe Map of circa 1848 shows "Toll House and Garden" on area 122a, near to the Stracey Arms Public House. The Owner is given as Charles Cory and the occupier as Philip Dowe, who is presumably the toll collector. In the census returns for Tunstall there is in 1851 John Ward, age 75, listed as the

Turnpike Gate Keeper, and in 1861 William Ashby, age 24, listed as Tollgate Keeper.

The Halvergate Tithe Map also has marked on area 288a a cottage listed as owned by the Turnpike Trustees and occupied by William Brooks. The 1841 Halvergate census lists Robert Brooks, age 55, as the Toll Collector.

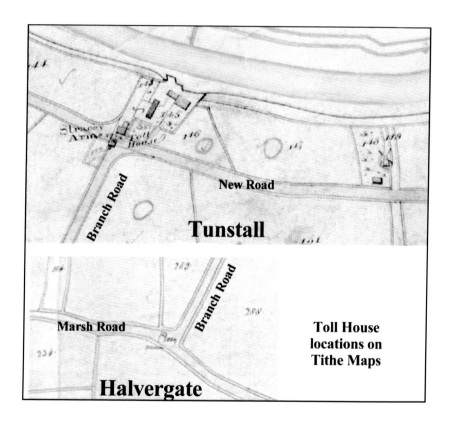

New Road

Branch Road

Tunstall

Marsh Road

Branch Road

Toll House locations on Tithe Maps

Halvergate

# AGRICULTURE AND FARMING

As a rural area both Halvergate and Tunstall were farming areas and remained so even after the industrial revolution. Farming was the main form of employment for most of the male population of the villages and remained so well into the twentieth century.

The old directories list Halvergate's soil as "mixed, subsoil, clay and brick-earth" and the soil at Tunstall as "mixed, subsoil, sand and clay". The chief crops grown in the area were, according to the old directories, wheat, oats and barley, and following the coming of the Cantley sugar factor in the 1920s, the growing of sugar beet became important to the region.

Almost two thirds of the combined old parishes of Halvergate and Tunstall were marshland and these marshes provided rich grasslands for fattening cattle, which were brought to marsh from other areas of the country. In the 1960s many of the marshes were ploughed but some marshes still have cattle and sheep grazing on them.

## FARMERS AT HALVERGATE
This list shows farmers at Halvergate who have been listed in various directories, census returns, and voter registers etc.

| NAME | DATES LISTED | NOTES |
|---|---|---|
| John Gillett | 1768 & 1806 | From Poll books. |
| William Gillett | 1802 & 1806 | From Poll books. |
| Robert Bately | 1806 | From Poll book. |
| John Davey | 1806 | From Poll book. |
| Cyrus Gillett | 1830/40s | Living at Markshall. (near Caistor St. Edmunds) |
| Richard Gillett | 1836 - 1861 | Age 65 in 1851, 270 acres, employs 10 |
| William Gillett | 1845 - 1877 | Age 36 in 1851, 330 acres. |
| Robert Gillett | 1845 - 1892 | Age 46 in 1861, 1200 acres, employs 57 labourers A shepherd 16 boys & a wheelwright. |
| Edward Dawdy | 1832 - 1851 | Age 60, in 1851, 120 acres. |
| Robert Howard | 1836 - 1854 | The Rookery, age 55 in 1851. |
| John Gillett | 1854 - 1861 | Age 45 in 1861, 300 acres, employs 8 men & 4 boys. |
| James Rushmer | 1845 | |
| Henry Sharman | 1845 | |
| Robert Walnes | 1845 | |
| Benjamin Howard | 1845 - 1861 | On the marshes. |
| Robert Ives | 1854 - 1865 | |

| | | |
|---|---|---|
| John Crowe | 1868/69 | |
| William Crowe | 1869 | |
| Robert Moore | 1868/69 | |
| Edward Smith | 1869 | |
| Robert Boult | 1877 | |
| George Thaxter | 1861 | Age 33. farmed 7 acres |
| Robert Howard Gillett | 1891 - 1912 | The Rookery, Age 66 in 1911 |
| George Youngs | 1904 | |
| Robert Bloom | 1904 - 1929 | Halvergate House. Age 70 in 1911 |
| Edward Phillipo | 1911 | Cattle Dealer, age 69. |
| Cyrus Doyle Gillett | 1916 - 1922 | |
| Frank Youngs | 1912 | Also grocer & PO. |
| John Harper | 1922 - 1937 | Crowes Farm. |
| Myrus Sutton | 1922 - 1937 | Halvergate Hall. |
| Albert Fred Watts | 1911 - 1922 | Nr. Crowes Farm, age 48 in 1911. |
| East Anglian Real Property Co. Ltd. | 1929 - 1937 | The Rookery Farm. (Mr Van Rossum) |

## FARMERS AT TUNSTALL

This list shows farmers at Tunstall which have been listed in various directories, census returns, and voter registers.

| NAME | DATE LISTED | NOTES |
|---|---|---|
| Thomas Boult | 1836 & 1848 | Near Church  50/- occupier in 1840. Near the Knoll on Tithe. Landowner Edward Rising Boult |
| James Pollard Skinner | 1836 - 1871 | Age 34 in 1851 farming 263 acres at Staithe Farm (owner Stephen Bately). 312 acres in 1861. |
| James C Skinner | 1881 & 1883 | Age 32 in 1881 farming 300 acres. |
| Richard Gillett | 1848  1854 | Tithe Map occupier of Fountaine's farmland. |
| Benjamin W. Rising | 1863/64 | Lower Farm |
| Robert Boult | 1867 & 1877 | £50 occupier of Lower Farm, living at Moulton. |
| Robert John More | 1867 & 1877 | £50 occupier of Fountaine's Farm, living in Fressingfield |
| Daniel C. Gillett | 1881 | Age 56, single, 430 acres, employs 11 men, 1 boy, 4 women |
| William Gillett | 1883 | Church Farm |
| Mrs Caroline A. More | 1883 & 1891 | Church Farm, Widow of R.J.More & daughter of Richard Gillett. |

| Robert John More | 1892 - 1937 | Son of R.J. and Caroline More. Listed At Church Farm and then Manor & Hall Farms. |
|---|---|---|
| Mrs Sophia Bullard | 1879 | |
| Henry Waters | 1881 & 1904 | Age 45 in 1881 near Church farm 200 acres. |
| George John Bates | 1887 & 1896 | Staithe Farm. |
| Fred Jones | 1900 | Occupier at Staithe Farm. |
| Robert Key | 1902 & 1912 | Staithe Farm, age 55 in 1911 |
| Benjamin Ch. Sutton | 1900 | Occupier Staithe Farm, but living at Freethorpe. |
| Scurrell Youngs | 1904 & 1912 | Marsh farmer at Boat Dyke Farm. Age 75 in 1911. |
| William Johnson | 1911 &1912 | Tunstall Hall, age66 in 1911. |
| Albert Watts | 1911 | Farmer & Market Gardener. |
| Arthur Shearing | 1945 | Staithe Farm. |

## COWKEEPERS

Many residents kept cows as the census and directories show. Some people kept a few cows right up into the mid to late twentieth century. In the early twentieth century and up until the 1970s the milk collected was put into churns for collection by the Milk Marketing Board. In the 1970s all cow-keepers were forced to have large tanks for their milk so most of the small milk producers gave up leaving only the larger farms supplying milk.

Some Cow-keepers listed in the early directories include:

| Name | Dates listed |
|---|---|
| Ben Howard | 1883 |
| John Carter | 1883 & 1892 |
| James Mutton jn. | 1890 |
| Fred Mutton | 1892 & 1929 |
| Ben Beck | 1912 |
| Mary Ann Phillipo | 1912 |
| James Thomas High | 1912 & 1929 |
| Wesley Stone | 1922 & 1929 |
| Robert Fransham | 1929 |
| | |
| | |

Some milk producers from the parishes in the early and mid 1900s included Sid Brister, Myrus Sutton, Walter Mallett, Sidney Mallett, John Lake, Brian Rowland, 'Pie' Beck, R J More, Fred Mutton, Arthur Key, Horace Beck, Maurice Mallett and Frank Harper.

Des Sharman recalls that Frank Harper was the first of the small cow-keepers to have his own milking parlour in the village.

## VETERINARY SURGEONS.

Halvergate for some years had a resident Veterinary surgeon.
Daniel John Hunting was listed here in the 1861 census and through till 1891.
A William Ives was also listed in 1861 and John Barr in 1892 and 1896.

**Elsie High on the marshes by High's Mill in the 1940s bringing cows in to be milked. From Bertie High.**

**Halvergate man, John Willimott, reedcutting.**

# THE MAIN FARMS ACROSS THE PARISH

## THE ROOKERY ESTATE

On the Halvergate tithe map the owner and occupier of the buildings and estate was given as Robert Howard who was a large landowner in the parish. The house was listed as the 'HALL' and was on area 79; and the adjacent area, 78, was listed as 'Farmyard and Offices'. The grade II listed house, located at TG41821068867, is believed to have been built around 1840, and is built of brick with a slate roof. The earlier Bryant's map, however, shows a farm and buildings at this location.

**The Rookery circa 1930.**

In the 1911 census the property was recorded as having eleven rooms, excluding any scullery, landing, lobby, closet, bathroom, office, shop and warehouses etc.

The Rookery Estate was sold in 1923 and became the property of the East Anglian Real Property Company Ltd. who were the instigators of the growing of sugar beet in the neighbourhood and who started Cantley Sugar Factory.

The Rookery was sold in 2001 for around £490,000.
Mr Michael Strauss was listed as the occupant of the Rookery in 2011.

Some Occupiers of the Rookery from census returns and directories were:

12

| Name of Occupant | Date Listed | Notes / Comments |
|---|---|---|
| Robert Howard | 1836 - 1854 | Marked as 'The Hall'. He was aged 55, a Farmer in 1851. |
| Susannah Daniels | 1861 | Age 25 listed at the Hall. |
| Edmund Broughton Knowles Lacon | 1869 & 1871 | Listed as the 'Hall'. Age 28 in 1871, banker & magistrate. |
| Robert Boult | 1883 | |
| Robert Howard Gillett | 1891 &1911 | Farmer age 46 in1891. |
| Mrs Gillett | 1912 | |
| | 1923 | Estate For Sale. |
| Van Rossum | 1929 | Director of the East Anglian Real Property Company Ltd. |

## HALVERGATE HOUSE FARM

This is a Grade II listed building located at about TG4198607221 on the west side of Squires Road. It is White Gualt brick and Red brick construction with a slate roof. The building is thought to have been built around 1840.

This building was marked on the Tithe Map of circa 1840, at area 85 as 'Dwelling & Offices' and was shown as owned and occupied by William Gillett. He was listed in 1845 White's directory as a 'Gent' The building was marked on the old OS maps as 'Halvergate House'. Bryant's Map of circa 1820 shows a building near this location marked as 'White House', suggesting an old building was demolished and rebuilt.

The Halvergate House estate with 117 acre, and including 3 cottages and a house, was put up for sale at the Star Hotel Great Yarmouth on 16 June 1886. (ref: NRO/ MC 527/17)

The 1911 census returns shows that it had ten rooms.

Halvergate House Farm, now stated as 115 a 3r 2p, was again put up for auction on 6th June 1914 at the Royal Hotel. The house was described as having a total of six bedrooms, a cellar, and in the yard outside were soft and hard water pumps, a wash or brew house, privy, and coalhouse. The tenant at that time was Robert Bloom. (ref: NRO/MC180/50) Mr R. J. More bought the property for about £2,800.

Some past occupiers or owners of the property include:

William Gillett listed in 1832 and 1868 directories (age 50 in 1841).

Robert Howard Gillett listed in 1883 as occupier with William Gillett as the owner.

Robert Bloom listed in 1911 as aged 70 a tenant farmer (died in 1929).

R. J. More, owner and farmer of about 700 acres.

The present occupant is Charles Reader, a director of the Wildfowlers association.

## HALVERGATE HALL FARM

Located at TG4199806579, this is a Grade II listed large white brick building. It was not shown on the Tithe Map of circa 1840 so the Hall was built after that time. This mansion was built for the local farming Gillett family.
The 1911 census records that the Hall had twelve rooms.
The Hall, and 8 acres, was put up for sale by auction in 1979.
It was put up for sale again in 2010 with an asking price £1,350,000.

| Name | Date listed | Notes / Comments |
|------|-------------|------------------|
| | | |
| Robert Gillett | 1869 - 1892 | Listed as **'New Hall'** Farmer, age 76 in 1891. |
| Thomas Kidner | 1896 | Famer |
| Mrs Kidner | 1911& 1912 | Age 72 in 1911. |
| Myrus Sutton | 1922 & 1937 | Farmer & Cattle Dealer. |
| | 1970s | Briefly unoccupied and then let. |
| Robert Chase | 1979 - 2010 | Norwich City chairman & Businessman. |
| Prof. Dobson | 2010 | |
| | | |

**HALVERGATE HALL 1952**

Fete held on the Halvergate Hall grounds when Robert Chase lived here.

**Left: Dan Fransham, gardener at The Hall. Right: Gilbert Hewitt, steward for Myrus Sutton.**

**Photographs supplied by Joy Brock.**

MYRUS SUTTON'S FARMWORKERS & THEIR PARTNERS

16

PHOTOGRAPH OF MYRUS SUTTON'S FARM WORKERS & THEIR PARTNERS. Supplied by Charlie Carter.

Back Row from left: Edmund Fransham, Arthur Key, Mr & Mrs Fred Dawson, Cecil London, Mr & Mrs London, Mr & Mrs Nicholls, Mr & Mrs Woolsey, Mr & Mrs Gilbert, Mr Dawson, Isaac Mallett, Mr & Mrs Parker.

Second Row from top: Frank Farrow, Mr Sharman, Mr & Mrs Fred Howard, Mr & Mrs Mallett, Mr & Mrs W Brown, Mr & Mrs G Fransham, Mr & Mrs Herbert Brown, Sam Ellis, Mr Tovell, Mr & Mrs Springall, Chummy Mallett, W Lawn, Sam Ellis

Third Row: Mrs H Sharman, Hetty Carter, Mr & Mrs Harper, Mr & Mrs George Key, Mr & Mrs Myrus Sutton, Mark Waters, Mr & Mrs Edgar Mallett, Mr & Mrs Adam Mallett, Mrs Chummy Mallett

Front Row: Reggie Garwood, Dan Fransham, Jack Taylor, R Carter, Ernie Brown, Albert Nicholls, Mrs W Stone, Millie Read, Wes Stone, Albert London, Fred Howard, Frank Dawson, Fred 'Orkshire' Carter, Walter Carter, Harry Johnson.

## MYRUS SUTTON:

Myrus Sutton lived at Halvergate Hall from before 1922 until he died in 1956. He was a J.P. and a leader of the Methodist Church. As well as at Halvergate Hall, he farmed at Upton Hall, Panxworth Hall, Blofield and Manor Farm and Lower Green Farm in Freethorpe. At one time there were about one hundred employees. They received their wages on a Monday morning. This practice of being paid on Monday instead of the end of the week dated from the days when some men had drunk a lot at the weekend leaving little money to feed the family. The cash was collected at Barcleys Bank in Norwich and taken round to the six farms for the stewards to fill the pay packets.

After Mr Sutton died, Freethorpe Lower Green, which belonged to his sister, and Blofield farms were sold and Upton and Panxworth, which were rented from Norwich Union, were given up. The executors carried on farming Halvergate Hall Farm and Freethorpe Manor Farm until his widow Mrs Dorothy Sutton died in 1999.

His farms included a large area of Halvergate marshes and he imported thousands of Irish Cattle to be fattened and sold for beef.

Bob Mallett, Charlie Newson and Jack Jones at Tunstall in July 1927. From Heather Wright.

Bob Carter photographed by a Halvergate drainage mill. He was 100 years old in 1968. He worked on the farms for Gillett, Kidner and Sutton, and lived all his life at Halvergate. From Joy Brock.

Top: Lady black currant pickers on Mr More's farm in the 1930s. Holding the pram is May Newson.
Bottom: Ladies working on More's farm during the War Years in the 1940s: Edna Springall, Vera Carter, Mrs Tovell, Mabel Beck and May Newson.
Supplied by Heather Wright.

## MANOR HOUSE FARM.

This grade II listed farmhouse building of red brick with pantiled roof is located on the west side of Tunstall Street at TG 4166607921. It was built in 1783.
Bryant's Map indicates, at about this location, a building marked as Thaxter's Farm.

The farmhouse and outbuilding were shown on area 12 of the Halvergate Tithe Map, circa 1840, and were listed as a 'dwelling' occupied by Richard Gillett and owned by Andrew Fountaine. The farm was referred to as **Fountaine's Farm** in the 1840s, then later as **Church Farm** and eventually as **Manor Farm**.
The farm was later run by the More family who are descendants of Richard Gillett. The 1911 census records Manor House Farm as having nine rooms, occupied by R.J. More, farmer age 48.

In recent years some of the outbuildings have been converted to provide Bed and Breakfast accommodation and a barn has been used for camping.

**On R.J. More's Farm in the 1940s. From the left: Bob Willimott, Arthur Springall, Wilf Read, Dick Gibbs, Bob Mallett & Reg Tovell. Supplied by Heather Wright.**

### TUNSTALL HALL FARM TG4171407935

Located on the east side of Tunstall Road the house itself was actually located just inside the original Halvergate parish opposite the Manor House, while the associated farm buildings were in the old Tunstall parish. The Hall is built of red brick with a pantile roof. This is now a Grade II listed building and dates from 1815 and has a plaque with the date and the initials ERB. The Tunstall Tithe map shows the owner of area 74, in which the farm outbuildings are located, as Edward

Rising Boult so the initials on the Hall probably refer to the dwelling being built for him.

The Hall appears to have long been part of the above mentioned Church Farm, and was in possession of the Gillett and related More families.

More's Farm in the 1940s

William Johnson, a 66 year old widower, was a farmer living here at the Hall in 1911 census when the building was said to have eleven rooms.

Robert John More was listed as the farmer for both Manor and Hall farms in 1937.

Combine Harvester in 1952

## STAITHE FARM, TUNSTALL TG4142908553

This is a Grade II listed redbrick and tiled farmhouse believed to have been built around 1800.

The building here on Bryant's Map of circa1820 was marked as "**Low Farm**". The Tunstall Tithe Map of about 1848 shows the farmhouse on area 20, owned by Stephen Bately, a Gent of Caister, and occupied by James Pollard Skinner. Skinner was listed here as farming 312 acres and employing ten men in 1861. He died in 1871, and Jane Skinner his widow was resident in 1871. She was succeeded by James C. Skinner who was listed here in 1881. George John Bates lived at the farmhouse from about 1885 through to the late 1890s.

Benjamin Charles Sutton of Freethorpe took over the farm, and in 1900 Frederick Jones lived at the Staithe Farm farmhouse. Robert Key was the farmer for many years after about 1902. In the 1911 census returns Robert Key, age 55 is listed living here as a farmer, and gives the number of rooms at the property as 10. Arthur Shearing was farming here from about 1945.

## CROWES FARM, HALVERGATE TG424073

The farmhouse was shown on area 95 of the Halvergate Tithe Map as occupied by farmer James Rushmer and owned by Samuel Crow, a Gent of Southtown. Although the name of the farm has a different spelling, it is probably from the name of the then landowner, Samuel Crow. This is a pair of semi-detached brick and tiled houses.

Some later farmers here include George Youngs in 1900 and John Harper from about 1915. Harper owned the farm till 1947 when it was acquired by R. J. More. The farm house, however, was not always occupied by the farmer or owner. In 1891 it was occupied by agricultural labourers William and Christopher Ward and in 1911 by stockman Robert E. Mallett, and in 1915 by John Gravener. Reginald Carter was a later occupant. The farm was later owned by Miss M. J. More.

## DAWDY'S FARM HOUSE TG4205106723

This is believed to have been built in the 18<sup>th</sup> century on the site of an earlier 17<sup>th</sup> century house. It is of brick and thatch and is a Grade II listed building.

The name originates from its one time occupier Edward Dawdy who was listed here in the 1832 voters register and in the 1854 directory as a farmer. The Tithe Map and Apportionment of circa 1840 shows that the property was then owned by George Boult of Norwich.

## LOWER FARM, TUNSTALL TG423083

The farmhouse is located at the end of Lower Farm Road. This was shown on the early Bryant's Map as **Gillett's Farm**.

In the early 1860s it was farmed by Benjamin W. Rising and later by Robert Boult of Moulton.

## HEATHER WRIGHT REMEMBERS

I was born in Tunstall in September 1933 but moved to Halvergate early 1934 and have lived in the village all my life. I attended Halvergate School until the age of eleven so was there during the war years. If the siren went we all had to lie down in the corridor and have gas masks on, and a blanket covering over us. Mary Beck taught us until the age of 7 or 8, then Miss Wheeler who used to wear reading glasses over her ordinary ones. She was strict, if you spoke or did anything wrong you would have to stand on your form.

The school nurse used to come round every so often, to look in your head for nits and ask if you had any itching scars or pimples. Also there was the dentist, who parked a caravan in the playground: everybody was terrified when we saw that coming. At the age of 11 it was off to Freethorpe School so we had to bike whatever the weather: Mr Rogers was the head master and was very strict. We had cooking classes once a week and the boys had carpentry. Other schools used to come for these lessons on different days. Miss Morrow was the cookery teacher and Mr O'Brian the carpentry master.

**1937 Coronation celebrations at the Street.
Supplied by Heather Wright.**

There was a Youth Club in the Village Hall, held once a week for darts, table tennis, billiards and cards, and they organised an outing once a year.

I got married in 1958 and have lived here at Crows Farm ever since.


## CHRISTINE SPARROW (NEE THACKER) REMEMBERS.

I was born at Halvergate in October 1948. My Family have lived in the parish of Halvergate for at least five generations. Sydney George Brister, my great grandfather, was a carpenter and wheelwright on Marsh Road; he was married to Phoebe (Howard Mutton). His son Charles, my grandfather, worked for his father in the family business starting at the age of fourteen. He later worked as a painter for Mr H. Jones a builder of Halvergate and Mr B Hubbard of Reedham. On his retirement he was working for East Anglian Real Property. He married Ada.

23

**Top: Charles Brister circa 1924. Below: Family gathering for Mr & Mrs Brister's diamond wedding. Supplied by Christine Thacker.**

Howard from Freethorpe and they also lived on Marsh Road. Mrs Brister worked in service at The Rookery in Halvergate for Mr & Mrs Cyrus Gillett and they lived all of their married life in the village. Charles and Ada had four children one of which, Edna, was my mother. She married Albert Thacker and he worked for Mr Joe Kerry as a cowman at Church Farm Wickhampton in the 1950s. They lived on Marsh Road to begin with and when I was two years old we moved up to 7 Church Avenue.

My First memories begin with my early school days which like most children in the village at that time were at the primary school. The teachers were Mrs Forster and Mrs Allum. On very cold days in the winter we had a large open fire and we were treated to mugs of hot cocoa made from the school milk. Another memory of those early days in the 1950s was standing outside the school gate

**School Play at Halvergate Primary School circa1950s.**

**From left: Christine Thacker, Pamela Dack, Violet Mallett, Patricia Nicholls, obliterated!, Brenda Saunders. Trevor Patterson at the rear. Supplied by Christine Thacker.**

waving union jack flags as the Duke of Edinburgh drove past on his way to Cantley factory. We also had dancing classes using an old wind up gramophone and in 1956 my brother Paul was born and he also attended the school.

As well as weekday school I also went to the Methodist Sunday School, where each year we had an anniversary in the barn on Wickhampton Road and also bible studies with Mr Shearing at Staithe Farm in Tunstall. My mother used to do casual work for Mr Shearing riddling potatoes. I also went blackcurrant picking with my Grandmother and Mother in Tunstall. We used to do lots of our shopping in the village: there was the post office run buy the Youngs family who also used to deliver the milk, my brother Paul helped Edwin Youngs during the school holidays and Saturday mornings. There was a shop on Marsh Road run by the Marsden family, which later became Frenchs, and also Rowlands the drapers on Squires Road . Then there was the Red Lion public house which in those days was run by the Bond family and of course is still there today. Many other things were delivered to the door: Harold the baker brought the bread , Mr Dack from Freethorpe brought groceries, Mr Durrant delivered newspapers and we also had meat delivered from a local butcher.

**Christine Thacker and Wendy Mallet on Moulton Road in the 1950s. Church Avenue in the background.**

My brother Paul was born in 1956 at 7 Church Avenue and spent all his young life in the village, as well as attending the primary school he also went to the youth club which was held at the village hall on Moulton Road, he played football for Halvergate, as in later years did his son Lee. He Married Anne O'Halleron in 1978 and they moved to Pond Cottage in Tunstall before later moving to Acle, Paul died suddenly in 2011 aged 54.

Out of school time I would go with my Grandmother for long walks picking wild flowers. I spent many happy times after school, weekends and school holidays with my grandparents.

In 1970 I married Colin Sparrow at the Methodist Chapel, as were my parents and grandparents, and we moved to Oaklands Close which was recently completed and our son Craig was born there. Colin attended the Sunday School as a teacher taking Craig with him and became superintendent for a short time, and Craig was baptised at the Chapel. We left the village about five years later but still go back often, as we have friends there and our family are buried in the churchyard.

# HALVERGATE CORN WINDMILL

The tower of this derelict mill is located on the west side of Mill Road at about TG41600598. There has been scaffolding around the tower for about the last 5 years and the current owner Robert Self has intentions of bringing the mill back to working order. To the south of the mill lies the mill house.

The tower corn mill was a 50ft, 6 storey mill, built of red brick and bears a date stone of 1866, indicating it was built around that time. It had 4 pairs of stones and 2 flour mills. It was a patent sail mill and power was provided by 4 double shuttered sails struck by rack & pinion via a chain pole .The boat shaped cap had a petticoat, gallery and an 8 bladed fan. The tower had two doors and the windows were offset. A bakery was also on the premises.

In the spring of 1935 the wind turned the sails of the windmill backwards ie 'tailwinded', and the brake did not stop the sails turning. It overheated and caused the windmill to catch fire. The mill inside was burnt out and it was not restored.

The ground floor of the derelict mill was later used as a storage facility by the Claridge family, and when Arthur Edwards built his bungalow next to the mill he had a water tank in the top of the mill for several years.

An earlier postmill was located at this site for many years. This was shown on both Faden's Map and Bryant's Map. A mill and house was also marked on the Tithe Map dated about 1840. This was on area 193 which was, according to the Tithe Apportionment, owned by Edward Palmer and occupied by Edward Rushmer.

From the Norfolk Chronicle, 13th December 1806:
"To be Sold by Private Contract & entered upon immediately
A POST WINDMILL situated in the parish of Halvergate in the county of Norfolk, with two pair of French stones, one pair 5 ft., the other 4 ft. 6 ins. & flour mill complete. Also a roundhouse & granary over the same, with cottage & garden there unto adjoining. The above premises are freehold & in good repair. Apply to Mr. Robert Bately in the parish of Halvergate aforesaid"

Also from the Norfolk Chronicle of the 13th March 1819 we have:
"To Millers. To be Sold by Private Contract a Capital POST MILL with two pair of French Stones, Flour Mill & Jumper; together with a newly erected brick Dwelling house, garden, stable & necessary offices. All Freehold. Apply to Mr. John Larter, the proprietor, Halvergate, Norfolk. "

Norfolk Chronicle, 9th August 1851:
"Windmill in full trade. Dwelling House, Garden, Stables & Outbuildings Halvergate. Wm. Spelman & Sons. Have received instructions from the Proprietor to sell by Auction on Saturday 23 August 1851 at the Norfolk Hotel, Norwich, at 3 o'clock the following Freehold Estate situate in the Parish of Halvergate 4 miles from Acle, 3 from Reedham Station & 13 from Norwich.
A POST WINDMILL in full Trade driving two pairs of French Stones, with two new spring & two common sails, iron shaft new about 12 months since, flour mill & every fitting requisite for carrying on the business. The Mill stands well for wind in a neighbourhood calculated to command a continuance of the excellent trade that is now attached to her. Adjoining is a comfortable Dwelling House. Also stables, gig house, cow house, piggery, malthouse & other buildings & a productive Garden walled in to the north. The Property is in the occupation of Mr. John Hewitt. Particulars of Mr. F. Fox, Solr. Rampant Horse Street, Norwich or of the Auctioneers, Norwich & Yarmouth."

Norfolk News - 18th April 1885:
"Preliminary Announcement. Halvergate. Within three Miles of Reedham station.
A Recently-erected Powerful Freehold BRICK TOWER WINDMILL driving four
pairs of Stones & two Flour Mills, Bake Office, Granaries, Dwelling house &
convenient Premises. Clowes & Nash are favoured with directions from the
Proprietor to Sell the above desirable MILLING PROPERTY by Auction during
the month of May."

Norfolk Chronicle - 20th June 1885
"Halvergate Mill. To be SOLD or LET, the capital Brick Tower WIND MILL,
Bake office, Granary, Stores & other Buildings wherein a profitable business is
now carried on, as can be shown, together with DWELLING HOUSE & Garden.
Apply to Clowes & Nash, Auctioneers, Bank Chambers, Norwich."

Yarmouth Independent - 19th May 1917:
"Spelmans on instructions from the Executors of E. E. Trett, decd. will Sell by
Auction on 6 June 1917 at the Star Hotel, Great Yarmouth the following ….
At Halvergate. Well situated Halvergate Mill with bake office, dwelling house
etc."

| Name of Miller/Occupier | Notes | Dates listed |
|---|---|---|
| Benjamin King | Miller & freeholder (Poll Book) | 1802 |
| John Larter | Miller | 1806 - 1819 |
| James Rushmer | | 1819 - 1836 |
| Edward Rushmer | Age 31 in 1851census | 1844 - 1851 |
| John Hewitt | Age 26 in 1851 census | 1851 - 1856 |
| Jacob Crane | Age 24 in 1861 census | 1858 |
| Thomas Crane | Age 21 in 1861, brother of Jacob | 1861 |
| Thomas Crane | Age 24 in 1891 | 1891 |
| Joseph Sheppard | Age 22 in 1891, lodging with Crane | 1891 |
| Charles Jacob Mutton | Lived at the Reedham Ship. | 1896 |
| John Woodcock | Age 32 in 1901 | 1900 - 1904 |
| Walter Benjamin Wright | Age 35 in 1911, miller & baker | 1908 - 1937 |
| Claridge family | Lived at Mill House | 1949 - 1981 |
| T. F Billing | Lived in mill house. Applied to convert mill for residential use. | 1980s |
| Robert Self | Became owner of the mill. In 2013 applied to convert outbuildings for residential use. | 1990s |
| | | |

The mill house was put up for sale in 1996 and again in 2009.

**Sketch of Halvergate Corn Mill in working order.**

# PUBLIC HOUSES PAST AND PRESENT.

## HARE & HOUNDS

This public house was owned by Coltishall Brewery until it was sold in May 1796, described as "With a stable and small garden thereto belonging – copyhold to the Manor of Halvergate, Fine arbitrary, quit rent 1 shilling 10 ¾ d".

On the Tithe Map of circa 1840 it was shown on area 175 as being owned by Patteson & Co. and occupied by Elizabeth Wyand.

It was located on the south side of the Street almost opposite the village pond.

The 1911 census records give the number of rooms as seven.

The licence was removed ion 5th February 1934.

The table lists some occupants found in the licence registers and old directories.

| Occupant / Licensee | Date listed | Comments / Notes |
|---|---|---|
| | | |
| BENJAMIN WYAND | 1836 | |
| ELIZABETH WYAND | 1845 | Age 65 in 1841 |
| MRS HELENA SMITH | 1846 | **see note below. |
| BENJAMIN SMITH | 1851 & 1856 | & plumber |
| THOMAS WILKINS | 1858 | |
| HENRY HOOK | 1861 | Age 33, & bricklayer |
| BENJAMIN MACK | 1865 & 1871 | |
| JONATHAN TOOK | 1872 & 1877 | |
| ROBERT HARPER | 03.01.1881 | Age 51 in 1881 & blacksmith. |
| CHARLES FLOOD | 16.05.1887 | |
| JAMES TIGHT | 18.03.1889 | |
| FREDERICK BRADSHAW | 20.01.1890 | Age 27 in 1891 |
| SARAH ANN ELIZABETH BRADSHAW | 14.07.1913 | Till closure in 1934. |
| | | |

** Note: Helena Smith was listed in 1845 as a 'Beer Seller'. She was the wife of Samuel Smith the blacksmith and Samuel was listed in the Tithe of circa 1840 as owner and occupier of areas 173 and 174, house, premises, cottage and shop. These premises were immediately adjacent to the Hare & Hounds.

In 1840 the "Halvergate Steeple Chase" was advertised to be held 19th Marsh 1840. 'A handsome silver cup to be presented by the spirited landlord S. Smith of the Steeple Chase Inn'. So it appears that Samuel and Helena Smith ran a beer-house from the premises now known as the 'Blacksmiths Cottage' and next door to the Hare & Hounds before taking over the pub.

**Above; The Hare and Hounds**
**Below: The Crown**

## CROWN

This was a public house located on The Street at about TG416066.
It was owned by Mr Chapman Ives of Coltishall Brewery until it was sold in May
1796. It was lot 28 – "The lease of all that public house called the Crown, situate in
Halvergate, with appurtenances thereto belonging; of which the lease there will be
four years unexpired at Michaelmas next"

It was marked on the Tithe Map and Apportionment as area 72a owned by Patteson and Co. and occupied by John Lincoln.

After closure in 1887 it was bought by the local vicar and converted into the **Reading Room and Institute** which opened on 1 November 1888.

The Secretary of the Reading Room and Institute was listed in 1912 and 1916 directories as Arthur Rushbrook.

This is now a private dwelling known as **Crown House.**

In 2001 the dwelling was put up for sale for £75,000.

The table lists some occupants found in the licence registers and old directories.

| Occupant / Licensee | Dates listed | Notes |
|---|---|---|
| ROBERT WALNES | 1836 | & Shoemaker |
| JOHN LINCOLN | 1841 -1851 | & shepherd 1841. age 48 in 1851& gardener |
| ROBERT BROWNE | 1854 -1856 | & basket maker |
| BESSY BECK | 1858 | |
| GEORGE W LINCOLN | 1861 | Age 31& shepherd |
| ROBERT HARPER | 1865 -1877 | & blacksmith.Age41 in1871 |
| THOMAS RISEBOROUGH | 03.01.1881 | Age 31 & fishhawker |
| ROBERT CHARLES HARPER | 20.11.1882 | & Bootmaker |
| JOHN CHAPMAN | 19.11.1883 | Till closure in 1887 |

**RED LION**

This public house is located at TG42250698 on the north side of Marsh Road. It was shown on the Tithe Map of circa 1840 as area 135 owned by Samuel Crow, and occupied by Robert Warnes. It was later owned by Nathaniel Skipper and then by Steward & Patteson from about 1875. In later years it was owned by Watney Man, Brent Walker and then Pubmaster.

The 1911 census indicated that the premises had seven rooms.

Between 1995 and 2000 the local post office was located in the pub.

The table lists some occupants found in the licence registers and old directories.

| Licensee / Occupants | Date listed | Notes |
|---|---|---|
| JOHN CARTER | 1836 | |
| ROBERT WARNES | 1841 | |
| ROBERT IVES | 1845 | |
| THOMAS SHARMAN | 1851 & 1865 | Age 57 in 1861 |
| JAMES SKIPPEN | 1868 | Age 38 in 1881 |
| ROBERT CHARLES HARPER | 19. 11. 1888 | Age 34 in 1891, & Shoemaker. |
| THURZA HARPER | 14. 02. 1927 | |
| WILLIAM YOUNG | 09. 05. 1927 | |
| CAROLINE ELLEN YOUNG | 27. 04. 1936 | |
| JAMES WILLIAM BOND | 14. 02. 1938 | |
| JOHN LOWTHER | c.1955 | Pub closed in 1978. |
| RONNIE SIMONDS | 1979 | |
| DAVID FRANCIS | 1982 | |
| WILLIAM PITCHERS | 1985 | |
| JANE PITCHERS | 1996 | |

Inside the Stracey Arms circa 1960
Edna Thacker behind the bar.

**Photo supplied by Christine Sparrow**

34

## STRACEY ARMS TG438090

This was originally the **STRACEY ARMS PUBLIC HOUSE** and lies to the south of the River Bure and adjacent to New Road. It is in the old parish of Tunstall. The name was altered to **THE THREE FEATHERS** in 1999 and later it became the **PONTIAC ROADHOUSE**. In October 2007 it was put up for sale with an asking price of oiro £750,000 and remained closed for a few years till it was reopened as a Spanish restaurant.

A building was marked here on the 1797, 1826 and first edition OS map of 1830's as **'SEVEN MILE HOUSE'**. It is probable that it first became a public house in the 1830s after the New Road was built.

It was marked on the Tithe Map as **'Stracey Arms'** on area 145, the owner was Edward Stracey and the occupier at that time was Christmas Francis.

It has probably been altered and rebuilt several times. The present buildings were built in the 1960s.

The 1911 census gives the number of rooms as eight.

BLOFIELD & WALSHAM LICENCE REGISTERS list this as an Alehouse. Some past owners include: Sir HENRY STRACEY of Rackheath, Sir EDWARD STRACEY of Rackheath, BULLARDS by 1903 and WATNEY MANN on 4th April 1967.

The table lists some occupants found in the licence registers and old directories.

| Licensees / Occupants | Comments | Dates |
|---|---|---|
| ROBERT CROWE | victualler | 1836 |
| CHRISTMAS FRANCIS | Aged 49 in 1851. | 1841 |
| JOSEPH POWLEY | | 1854 |
| JOHN POWLEY | | 1856 |
| JAMES WILKINS | Age 33 in 1861. | 1858 - 1861 |
| THOMAS ENGLAND SAMSON | | 1864 |
| SCURRELL YOUNGS | Aged 33 in 1871, & a farmer of 18 acres. | 1868 |
| WALTER THURTLE | | 13.05.1889 |
| HENRY SPENCER RAYNER | Aged 25 in 1891. | 19.01.1891 |
| THOMAS BRINDID | | 06.07.1891 |
| JOHN ROBERT LUBBOCK | | 12.11.1900 |
| BENJAMIN EDWARD ALLEN | Aged 41 in 1911, Publican & Dealer. | 18.11.1907 |
| ROBERT MARTIN MALLETT | | 13.01.1919 |
| GEORGE MOLL | | 17.05.1920 |
| DAVID ALFRED WILLIAM | | 14.11.1921 |

| EASTER | | |
|---|---|---|
| EDWARD JOHN BRUNSON | | 15.05.1922 |
| HANNAH BRUNSON | | 04.02.1935 |
| JOHN WILLIAM MUSKETT | | 24.06.1935 |
| BENJAMIN EDWARD BLAKE | | 23.03.1953 |
| ALEX BABLOT | | 09.04.1962 |
| EDWARD KENDLE THACKERAY | | 29.11.1965 |
| JOHN CYRIL GREEN | | 13.06.1966 |
| EDWARD KENDLE THACKERAY | | 06.02.1967 |
| SAMUEL JOSEPH CHAPMAN | | 25.03.1968 |
| EDWARD KENDLE THACKERAY | | 06.01.1969 |
| ALAN HULME | | 24.11.1969 |
| COLIN ERNEST HOWES | | 31.03.1970 |
| JOHN LEONARD BURCHALL | | 12.02.1973 |

**Stracey Arms Public House.**

**Left: Scurrell and Elizabeth Youngs and family outside the Stracey Arms circa 1880. The children are believed to be Sarah, Betsy and Jane, and the baby Benjamin Youngs.**

**Below: Scurrell Youngs with members of the family believed to be on the Acle New Road.**

**Photographs supplied by John Youngs.**

**A group of elderly Youngs family members taken in 1928;
From the left: Scurrell age 91, George age 89, William age 80
and seated Betsy, age 85. Supplied by Joy Brock.**

# CHURCH OF ST PETER AND ST PAUL, HALVERGATE TG4175406691

This is a Grade I listed building; first listed in September 1962. The Church was built in the 13th century when Halvergate village was on the then great estuary of the River Yare. The roll call of incumbents displayed in the Church dates back to 1293. The Abbots of Tintern were the early patrons but in the 13th & 14th centuries patronage passed to the King and later the Bishop of Ely. It now rests with the Bishop of Norwich.

THE CHURCH, HALVERGATE.

This medieval parish church was restored by Brown and Lowe in about 1857, a new porch was built in 1867 by James Benest, and a new roof was made by R.M. Phipson in 1873.

It was built of flint with stone dressings and slate roof. It consists of a West tower, south porch, nave and chancel. The tower is believed to date from about 1450. The doorway is believed to be 14th century and the chancel 19th century.

The Organ was made by Norman and Beard and installed in 1906 and cost £200.

**Whites's 1883 Directory** gave the following description:

*"The Church, is an ancient fabric of flint with stone quoins. It consists of nave, chancel, south porch, and square tower. The latter is 84 feet high, and commands and extensive view; it is of the Perpendicular style, contains a peal of six bells, and is surmounted by figures of the four evangelists. Here are several tablets of the Gillett and Bately families. In 1852 the tower was restored at a cost of £300; in 1857 the church was re-seated with neat open benches; in 1862 new windows were*

*inserted; and in 1877 the chancel was rebuilt and the nave newly roofed. The tower has some pretty specimens of 'sound' holes."*

In 1971 the Halvergate and Tunstall churches became part of the Freethorpe Benefice along with Wickhampton church.

**Postcard View of the Vicarage circa 1930.**

The Old Vicarage, located opposite the church on The Street, is built of brick with a slate roof. This is believed to have been built around the mid-1850s and with a separate Coach-house, and on the site of a former parsonage. The 1854 directory states that "A new vicarage is in course of erection near the church". On the Tithe Map of circa 1840 the rectory was shown on area 179, opposite the church, and in the occupation of the Rev. George Burges.

When no longer required by the church the Vicarage was sold off as a private dwelling and remains so today.
    In 1990 the old vicarage and the associated coach-house were put up for sale at £295,000. In 2006 the vicarage along with a now 'converted' coach house and an outdoor swimming pool was put up for sale with an asking price of £680,000.
The latest occupants were Mr and Mrs David Jones.

# REMAINS OF CHURCH OF ST. PETER AND ST. PAUL TUNSTALL.

**TUNSTALL**

This is located at TG41705080021on Low Farm Road, and was listed on 25-9-62 as Grade II building.

The parish church at Tunstall is believed to have been built in the 14th century on the site of an earlier church. The register dates from 1577. Apart from the chancel and a 19th century vestry, the building is in ruins, believed to have fallen into disuse after the nave roof collapsed in 1660. It was constructed of Flint with brick and stone dressings and the Chancel is roofed with slate. Some repairs were carried out in 1705, and more in1853. A plaque in the chancel arch reads *'This rebuilt by Mrs Elizabeth Jenkenson, the relict of Miles Jenkenson, Tunstal Esq. and Ms Anne Kelkall, daughter of Miles and Elizabeth. 1705.'*

In 1980 the church was made redundant but a Trust was formed to preserve the building.

The last marriage at Tunstall church was that of Les Mallett and Gloria Beck in1961.

**Postcard View of the Tunstall Church circa 1930.**

There is a Legend concerning the church:

*When the church was destroyed by a fire, the timbers of the bell chamber were destroyed, so the bells fell down but were unharmed. The parish priest decided to keep them for his own covetous purposes. The churchwardens also decided they should have the bells and could sell them and share the spoils between them. Their plans were discovered by the priest, and an angry feud ensued when the parties met in the church. Each party tried to get possession of the bells, and, as they quarrelled the devil appeared on the scene, and instantly seized the bells and made off. The priest and churchwardens, forgetting their dispute, set off in pursuit but the thief vanished from their sight, diving straight through the earth and taking the bells with him. Where he disappeared, they saw a dark pool of water with bubbles rising to the surface. The bubbles appeared for many days and years after, and the bells were lost at the bottom of the pit. The pool obtained the name of Hell Hole, and the clump of alders above it was long known as Hell Carr.*

## HALVERGATE METHODIST CHAPEL

**Postcard view of the chapel.**

The Primitive Methodist Chapel is located at TG42210705 and was built in 1878 at a cost of £550. It has a school room .and was on the Acle Circuit.

Some local resident ministers listed in the 1891 census returns include John Fransham and John Gaze.

**Mabel Sutton opening the Halvergate Methodist Chapel in July 1948 after it had been redecorated. Photograph supplied by Joy Brock.**

**Another gathering outside the Methodist Chapel in the 1950s. The man on the right is Arthur Shearing. Photograph supplied by Christine Sparrow.**

**Wedding Photo Taken by the Chapel, 9th July 1930. Back Row: Charles Brock, Anna Brock, George Youngs, Elizabeth Brock, Frank Youngs, Harriet Youngs, Robert Harper, Middle Row: Jessie Brock, Alec Brock, Ivy Brock, Amy Brock, Front Joyce Mallett, Joan Myhill.**

**Wedding photograph of Ernest Knights and Doris Youngs in 1940, taken by the village hall. Supplied by Joy Brock**

This cottage on Squires Road was once a shop run by the Rowland Family. Mrs Rowland ran the shop and Mr Rowland had a cycle business opposite the shop.

Mr Brian K. Rowland on his home made bike going around the villages with his wares.

## HALVERGATE SHOPKEEPERS

Although there is an absence of shops today, the village has had a number of shops in the past. No shopkeepers were listed in the Tunstall census returns and directories. The following are from census returns and directories etc.

| NAME | DATES LISTED | NOTES |
| --- | --- | --- |
| Edward Jones | 1836 & 1854 | Shopkeeper & carpenter |
| Edward Palmer | 1836 | |
| William Belson | 1845 | |
| Robert Saint | 1854 | |
| John Harper | 1854 | Grocer & Blacksmith |

| Sarah Ives | 1854 & 1861 | Age 65 in 1861, grocers shop |
|---|---|---|
| Harriet Jones | 1861 | Age 63 in 1861, grocers shop |
| Nathaniel Skipper | 1868 & 1877 | & pork butcher. |
| George Mallett | 1868 - 1904 | Grocer, draper, butcher, & market gardener, age58 in 1891. |
| John Gaze | 1883 & 1900 | & Post Office, butcher & carpenter. Age 28 in 1881. Also a Methodist Preacher. |
| Georgiana Rowland | 1890 & 1891 | Age 62 in 1891. |
| Frank Ernest Youngs | 1904 - 1937 | Grocer, Butcher & Post Office. The Street. Age 32 in 1911. |
| Walter William Jermy | 1911 - 1937 | Age 34 in 1911 Grocer on Marsh Road |
| Mr & Mrs B. K. Rowland | 1930s | Drapers, Grocery and cycle workshop on Squires Road. |
| Eddie Young | 1940s | Post Office etc. |
| Mr & Mrs Marsden | 1950s | Marsh Road |
| French | 1960s | Marsh Road. |
| Mr Pitcher | c. 1990 | Shop & post office. |
|  |  |  |

## HALVERGATE POST OFFICE

The earliest mention of a Halvergate post office is in the 1854 directory. Tunstall has never had its own Post Office. This was located at the house of the then schoolmaster, a Mr John Lemon. The location of that house is not known. Subsequent directories do not mention a post office until the 1883 directory which lists John Gaze at the post office. This was located on the north side of the Street, at the site now known as The Old Post Office, TG4202306783. This location on the Tithe Map of circa 1840 was area 130, listed as house and premises, owned by Edward Palmer and occupied by James Beck, who was a bricklayer at that time.

Mr Frank Youngs took over the Post Office around 1904. The Youngs family also kept cows and delivered milk around the village. Eddie Youngs took over from his father Frank.

The 1868 directory records "letters through Acle which is the nearest Money Order office".
The 1877 directory says that Acle is the nearest Money order and Telegraph Office.
The 1890 directory puts Acle as the nearest Money Order and Telegraph Office, and states "letters arrive 7:25 am and depart at 3:20pm, via Norwich"

In the 1896 directory: "Letters through Norwich arrive at 7:15am; dispatched at 7:5am &3:40pm; there is no Sunday post. Postal Orders are issued here, but not paid. Acle is the nearest money order & telegraph office."

The 1911 census returns also lists James Springall as a 'Rural Letter Carrier' and Elsie Harper as a 'Post Office Messenger'.

The old Post Office closed in the 1980s.
Mr Pitchers ran a post office service from the Red Lion pub between 1994 and 2000. There is now no Post Office in the village.

The Old Post Office is a detached red brick building with a slate roof, and is now a Grade II listed building.

In the year 2000 the former post office building was put up for sale with a price of £225,000, it was again up for sale in 2005 for £289,950 and sold again in 2007 for about £310,000.

**Elsie Springall with Doris and Amy Youngs at the Halvergate Post Office shop in 1912. Photograph supplied by Carol Hannant.**

**Top: Mr Eddie Youngs in July 1934 near the Post office. Bottom: Postcard view of the Halvergate Post Office. Supplied by Joy Brock**

## MY CHILDHOOD MEMORIES OF HALVERGATE BY CAROL HANNANT (NEE YOUNGS)

My earliest recollection of life in Halvergate was being hurriedly ushered along Bakers Road by my Mother to endure another day of Schooling at the Village School. Unlike some of the other children, my idea of a happy day was being at home with my Dad on the Farm not being cooped up all day in a School Class Room. However, I must have adjusted to this new way of life as latter memories of school days are of friendships and fun.

I remember my infant teacher as Mrs. Foster who lived in Squires Road and the School headmistress as Miss Wheeler. She also lived in the Village but had an air of authority about her which meant that children didn't cross paths with her if it was at all possible not to.

An after school adventure with a group of friends stays in my memory mainly because of the wrath of Miss Wheeler the following day. Rather daringly, we had been scrumping apples in an orchard next to Miss Wheeler's home unaware that she had been listening to our antics from her garden. The following day, our names were called out in front of the whole school and we were chastised with a severe warning and a punishment of many missed play times. We were much more careful about after school activities after that.

Sunday School was a much happier occasion with lots of singing and spiritual guidance from Mr. Frank Carter, Mr. Dan Fransham, Mr. John Fransham, 'Aunt' Audrey Carter and 'Aunt' Muriel Wright. The highlight of the year was the Sunday School Anniversary held in Mr. Sutton's barn on Wickhampton Road. The barn would be scrubbed and the walls whitened in preparation for the big day. Some years, the barn was so full that people would be standing at the back. After many weeks of rehearsing new hymns and recitations, the day couldn't come quick enough for me. My Mum had cooked meat and made trifles for all the family who would come over for the afternoon and evening services. I even remember when we had two sittings for tea as there were too many to sit down all at once. Definitely, no buffets in those days. All the girls on the platform had new frocks for the occasion and the lads were very well groomed. Great excitement at the evening Service was the announcement of the 'collection'. Had we beaten Freethorpe this year? The reward for everyone's hard work was the Sunday School Outing which always headed to Lowestoft with a fish and chip tea in Gorleston. Some years two buses were filled with excited children and their parents all singing their heads off. Such good times.

I have such happy memories of my childhood at home with Mum and Dad (Queenie and Eddie Youngs) my brother Edwin and my Aunt Amy and Uncle Raymond all living at the Post Office Farm. Life was very busy in those days with Dad milking his herd of Cows early in the morning. Then bottling the milk before heading off around the Village on his post bike to deliver the mail. After a hearty breakfast, he was off again in his van to deliver the milk to his customers. Following lunch, it was bottle washing and another session of Milking the Cows.

This left Aunt Amy in charge of the Post Office Shop and Mum busily cooking, housekeeping and helping out wherever she could. After leaving School, my job took me into the City but Edwin stayed on the Farm and ran the business when Dad finally retired. The Post Office Shop was an 'Aladdins Cave' of everything from Postage Stamps to Groceries, shoe polish and even Paraffin for lights and heaters. The Shop had been run by the Youngs Family since the late 1800's originally as a Butcher's Shop

**Queenie and Amy Youngs with Paul and Nicola pictured in the Post Office Shop just before its closure in 1980. Supplied by Carol Hannant**

and finally closed its doors in 1980

The Village has rightly changed so much over the years but I hope that the memories of today's children, although very different, will be just as happy as mine.

# HALVERGATE SCHOOL.

The National School and teachers residence was built in 1854 at about TG415065 on area 66 of the Tithe Map, on the south side of Moulton Road. Some school masters were listed in the village, however, prior to that time as the list below shows.

The National school was a red brick building, had three classrooms and was heated by a coal-fire. In 1894 the school was enlarged to take up to 130 children. It was again enlarged in1910/11.

The old National school was burnt down in February1929 and the older children were then sent to Freethorpe School while the juniors and infants had lessons in the Chapel.

The ruined school building was rebuilt and became the Village Hall and was also shown on some maps as the Church Hall. The Village Hall was used for club meetings and gatherings, and as a doctors surgery one morning each week. A box was placed outside the village hall where prescription medicines were placed for collection. A club licence was granted in 1978 to the village hall.

A new primary school was built near the corner of Marsh Road and Squires Road and this eventually closed in 1988, and was sold and became a residential property. This property is now run as a guesthouse.

This lists some Halvergate teachers from census returns and directories etc:

| NAME | DATE LISTED | COMMENTS |
| --- | --- | --- |
| Benjamin Wyand | 1806 | School master |
| Thomas Callow | c. 1830 | School master |
| Joseph Turner | 1836 & 1845 | School master |
| John Lemon | 1854 | School master & also post office. |
| Elizabeth Harper | 1861 | School teacher, age 19 |
| Mary A. Solomon | 1861 | Age 26, School mistress |
| Eliza Mallett | 1861 | School mistress, age 20 |
| Sarah Ann Oliver | 1862 - 1869 | Nat School Mistress |
| Emma Darnell | 1871 | Cert School Mistress age 24 |
| | | |
| Miss Harriet Creme | 1883 | |
| Eva May Goodchild | 1890 & 1892 | Age 30 in 1891, School Mistress |
| Kate Marian Howard | 1891 | Age 25, assistant teacher |
| Charlotte Carter | 1891 | Age 23, teacher. |
| Ella Rands | 1896 | School mistress. |
| | | |
| Victoria Caleby | 1900 & 1904 | School Mistress. |

| Althea Bradshaw | 1911 | Age 20, teacher. |
|---|---|---|
| Robert Rose | 1911 - 1916 | School Master |
| Mary Beck | 1911 -1940s | Age 32 in 1911, school teacher |
| Agnes Jane Gentry | 1922 | |
| Mr Rogers | 1920s | |
| Miss Wheeler | 1930s 40s | Head teacher |
| Mrs Barbara Foster | 1930s  50s | Teacher |
| Mrs Boast | 1940s | |
| Mrs Allum | 1950s | Teacher |
| Mrs Waklin | 1970s | Teacher |
| Eric Green | 1967 -closure | Head teacher. |

**Halvergate School Football Team in 1923.**

# Halvergate School Photographs from 1915

School Concert

School Concert circa 1915

**Photographs from Gertie Springhall's time at Halvergate School. Supplied by Rodney Howard. Top: School concerts Bottom: Left Gertie in school dress, Right Gertie growing up.**

54

**School Pantomime: Ursula Mutton, Elizabeth Grigglestone, Judith Harper, Patricia Nicholls,Daphne Sharman, Rita Carter, Rita Willimott, Janet Lake, Rosalle Shorten, Pamela Dack & Glenda Newson**

**21 February 1929 School after the fire.**

**Photographs supplied by Joy Brock.**

56

## CARPENTERS & JOINERS.

| NAME | DATE LISTED | NOTES |
|---|---|---|
| Samuel Wyand | 1836 | Joiner |
| John Gooch | 1836 | |
| Robert Gooch | 1836 | |
| Edward Jones | 1836 & 1854 | |
| Robert Mallett | 1845 - 1861 | Age 87 in 1861 |
| Robert Mallett | 1861 - 1900 | Age 25 in 1861 |
| James Stout | 1861 | & wheelwright |
| Samuel R. Saint | 1861 | Apprentice, age18 |
| Jonathan Skippen | 1861 | Age 30. |
| | | |
| John Gaze | 1881 & 1891 | & grocer |
| William Knights | 1891 & 1929 | Age 33 in 1891. In the City |
| William Knights jn. | 1911 | Age 22 in 1911. |
| John. C. Harper | 1891 & 1937 | Apprentice in 1891 |
| Sidney Brister | 1916 & 1937 | & Wheelwright |
| William M. Garwood | 1911 | Wheelwright, age 28 |
| | | |

Jack Harper

**Sidney George Brister, Carpenter & Wheelwright.**

## CARRIERS & TRANSPORT.

| NAME | DATE LISTED | NOTES |
| --- | --- | --- |
| John Moll | 1861 | Agricultural Carter |
| Philip Wyand | 1861 & 1869 | Carrier, age 56 in 1861 |
| Henry Waters jnr. | 1911- 1916 | Carrier & Market gardener. Age 43 in 1911 on Bakers Road. |
| Frank Youngs | 1916 - 1929 | Carrier to Gt. Yarmouth, grocer and sub postmaster etc. |
| Brian Kenneth Rowland | 1922 - 1937 | Cycle Agent & draper etc. |
| Archie Jermy | 1929 - 1937 | City Corner. Motor Engineer & Haulier. |
| Lake | 1940s | Coaches to Gt. Yarmouth. |
| 'Chinky' Carter | | Haulier & Taxi service. |
| | | |

**Eddie Youngs and Sidney Springall at Motor Engineers at City Corner.**

## CHARLIE CARTER REMEMBERS;

Charlie is a great grandson of William Hewitt of Berney Arms (King Billy). Charlie's father, also Charlie Carter 'Chinky' had an old Ford truck in which Charlie often went with his father. When the people from the marshes at Berney Arms, The Halvergate Fleet and The Haddiscoe Island etc. moved house they would use Chinky's truck. One of the jobs they used the truck for was to go to Berney Arms to collect muck and take it to Reedham Nurseries.

'Chinky' Carter's truck. Standing: Charlie Carter, behind the wheel his bother Ivan Carter.
Below: 'Chinky' Carter's taxi, a 1923 Bewick.

**Paintings from Charlie Carter.**

Top: Derelict building in The City where Charlie Carter kept his pigs in the 1960s. The building was later demolished.
Bottom: A painting made by a soldier during WWII of Clay Cottage in The City. From Charlie Carter.

**Gathering at the Stracey Arms after weed cutting at the bottom of dykes. Back: John Willimott, Aubrey Hewitt, Basil Willimott, Charlie Carter, Gerry Mallett. Front: Royston Mallett and 'Spud' Mallett. Photo from Charlie Carter.**

Charlie recalls that his father did lantern slide shows in the old Crown House and that Brian Rowland went around the villages with a square box on the front of his bike selling clothing.

During the WWII years people collected newspapers and took them to a bullock shed opposite the War Memorial site for collection. The intended purpose was to keep up peoples spirits and to put the newspapers towards the purchase of a spitfire airplane for the war effort. The American forces in the area often went to the Sandhole to do their shooting practice. An American airplane, B24H Liberator, came down in Tunstall in July 1944 with 12 live 500lb bombs still onboard. It was buried in the marsh with only the tail visible. Some years later, in 1979, after the live bombs were unearthed by aviation enthusiasts, to blow up the bombs the authorities closed the Acle New Road and everyone in the villages were informed that they must open their windows.

The village hall was used for many purposes such as wedding receptions, dances and as the doctor's surgery and a baby clinic.

**1953 Coronation celebrations with Charlie Carter dressed as a woman.
Photograph supplied by Heather Wright.**

### GEORGE HAZELL REMEMBERS.

My mother, who had been a District Nurse on Foulness Island, took a similar post at Halvergate about 1935, when I was aged 4. My father had died after a motor-bike accident when I was 6 months old. For 4 years we lived in rented rooms with Dick Woodcock and his family at the White House. He had a small chicken farm.

In 1939 mother had a Boulton & Paul bungalow built on a plot between the mill and the twelve Council houses on Mill Road or "up the mill" generously supplied by farmer Myrus Sutton. We lived there until 1951 when I married and moved away to Gorleston, taking mother with us as by then she was bed-ridden with rheumatoid arthritis.

We had happy times at Halvergate school under Miss Wheeler. She would get us into a circle for a "spelling B", and one day the word was "sure". It went right round the ring, because we could not imagine it starting with anything else but "sh".

I later attended the CNS with Terry Beck, from Tunstall, who arranged for me to work during harvest for Mr R. J. More. It was all horse power then, except one small tractor that Terry drove. There was a young horse called "Snip", who had a ticklish back, and one day I was sitting on her back as she pulled a loaded tumbrel and she broke into a run. The men shouted "Get off her back!", so I jumped off into a shock of corn.

Much of my time was spent drag-raking, first between the shocks and later on cleared stubble. One job I dreaded was raking just north of Acle New

62

Road, having to cross both the road and the railway line. I am sure it took Wilfred and me with our two rakes longer to get there and back than to do the job. We had to pass through several gates, some of which were narrower than our rakes, especially mine which had huge wheels and hubs that stuck out about six inches. This meant dismounting and leading the horse at the head to get one wheel through, then, after several bites, the second. If a horse feels trapped it is likely to try to bolt so it was quite a harassing experience for a young greenhorn like me!

Mr More also grew lots of blackcurrants providing employment for scores of women in the picking season.

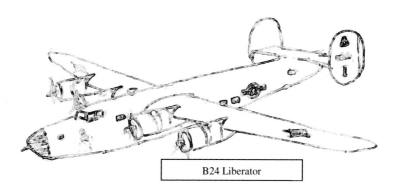

B24 Liberator

Meanwhile came the war, with its gas masks to carry to school in their cardboard boxes and a shoulder string, ration books and ID numbers, mine was TRBD16/2. One night it seems a "Molotov Bread Basket" exploded nearby scattering its incendiary bombs. Nine fell on Ben Wright's premises by the mill next door and two near number 1, the other side, all without serious damage. Another night we were outside when 5 or 6 planes went down in flames. We later learned they were Liberators returning from a raid followed by enemy fighters which shot them down as soon as they put their landing lights on.

A group of us children were playing on Mill Road one day when we spotted a barrage balloon approaching on a strong westerly wind. As it neared we saw its mooring cable dragging on the ground across Ben Wright's 6-acre field between the Council houses and the Red House. Now three power cables hung across the field from North to South so we had a sparky display that would have been brilliant at night.

I remember one incident in sport: during a football match I saw Sidney Springall, who lived "up the Mill", on or near the half-way line turn his back to the rival goal and sky the ball over his head, beating the goalie by the angle the ball fell!

Another memory about the church is that I used to pump the organ for a while and one day I fell asleep during the sermon. The poor organist got just one note towards the hymn, but it was enough to rouse me to pump frantically to enable play to resume!

As to characters in the village I remember that Noel Flint "Noky" always seemed to be M.C. for anything at the village hall and elsewhere. He lived in a little cottage by the pond. Amy and Eddie Youngs of the Post Office also put a lot into village life.

After some extreme weather, it may have been 1947, some of the marshes had flooded a few inches and then frozen, so a gang of us teenagers went down, some with skates, to explore. There must have been a wind frost, because the surface was covered with thin upright blades of ice. In places the ice was level across marsh and dyke, but happily it bore our weight.

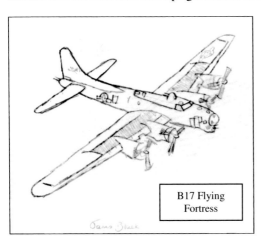

B17 Flying Fortress

Late one night I was stopped by Mr Race the village policeman for having no lights. I pleaded my innocence: that they were on when I left Great Yarmouth, but having cycled home against the wind they had gone out. It was the batteries' fault! It didn't wash and I had to pay up. I feel sure it was 10 shillings, or 50p today. I played him at billiards at the village hall, but I cannot remember ever beating him.

When I was 18 he came round to tell me I'd be picked up the next day because I had not registered for my National Service. I said, "Suppose I'm not here?" He replied I had better be here, or there would be worse trouble. We had become Jehovah's Witnesses by then, after Bert Harper had cycled from Yarmouth a time or two to reason from the scriptures with my mother through her bedroom window. Then Bob Smith and his blind wife Millie on their tandem and their son Derek on his bike came from Reedham weekly, even through the blackout and stray shrapnel to study the Bible with us. Since we were an International Christian Brotherhood our principle was neutrality in every nation.

Looking back over these recollections it seems that marshes were like a magnet to my mother; I was born in Bridgewater in the Somerset Levels. When I was 2 we moved to Foulness Island which is all marshes protected by a sea wall. Our next move to bring us closer to my grandparents at Oulton, was to Halvergate with extensive marshes. Finally we settled in Gorleston where our back entrance leads to Bell's Marsh Road!

## BUILDERS & BRICKLAYERS OF HALVERGATE.

The following are from census returns and directories

| NAME | DATE LISTED | NOTES |
|------|-------------|-------|
| James Beck snr. | 1845 | Age 60 in 1861 |
| James Beck jnr. | 1854 - 1917 | Age 31 in 1861 |
| Henry Hook | 1861 | Age 33 & Inn keeper at Hare & Hounds |
| James Mutton | 1868 -1896 | Age 75 in 1891 |
| George Mutton | 1891 | Age 46 |
| Daniel Jones | 1891 - 1911 | Age 36. in 1891. |
| Benjamin Mutton | 1891 | Age 35 |
| James Daniel | 1896 | |
| Benjamin Beck | 1891 - 1900 | & flour dealer & pork butcher age 44 in 1891 |
| Jeremiah Mutton | 1896 - 1912 | Age 39 in 1891 |
| Charles John Harper | 1912 | |
| Sidney Lawrence Wyand Mutton | 1916 - 1929 | |
| Edward Jones | 1912 - 1922 | |
| Harold Jones | 1929 | Lived at White House. |
| James Frederick 'Sticky' Mallett | 1937 | Also a chimney sweep. |
| | | |

## BLACKSMITHS

The blacksmith was an important member of the community in a rural village until well after the invention of the combustion engine and into the middle of the twentieth century.

| NAME | DATE LISTED | NOTES |
|------|-------------|-------|
| Samuel Smith | 1836 | |
| William Newton | 1836 | |
| James Rushmer | 1836 | |
| Robert Smith | 1845 | |
| Alfred Wyand | 1845 -1883 | |
| John Harper | 1854 -1883 | |
| Robert Thrower | 1861 | |
| Robert Alfred Harper | 1891 -1929 | Age 67 in 1911. The Street. |
| James Wyand | 1891 -1904 | |
| Alfred Wyand Beck | 1911 -1937 | Age 29 in 1911 Marsh Road. |
| C. J. Harper | 1911 | Age 43 in 1911. The Street. |
| Fred Sharman | 1937 | |

King Billy Hewitt on the left at the blacksmiths near the Red Lion Pub.
Second from the right is Alfred Beck, blacksmith.

Blacksmith's at Cat's Corner on the Street

## BOOT & SHOEMAKERS

Before the advent of the bicycle and motor transport the main means of getting about was by horse and on foot. Consequently boot and shoe-makers became important in remote rural villages.

| NAME | DATE LISTED | NOTES |
|---|---|---|
| Robert Walnes | 1836 | At Crown Inn. |
| Thomas Jones Sn. | 1836 -1861 | Age 77 in 1861. |
| Thomas Jones jn. | 1861 - 1877 | Age 48 in 1861. |
| James Mallett | 1836 - 1854 | |
| Charles Turner | 1836 - 1845 | |
| Robert Jones | 1861 | Age 33. |
| James Jones | 1868 -1877 | |
| Samuel Jones | 1883 -1896 | Age 71 in 1891. |
| Robert Skipper | 1891 | Apprentice, age 16. |
| Robert Harper | 1891 | Age 34 & Publican. |
| Albert Watts | 1904 - 1929 | |
| | | |

## OTHER OCCUPATIONS

Many other occupations were found in the two parishes. An indication of these for the 1861 and 1891 census returns is given later.

At various times there was listed in the census returns or directories a brick-maker, Thatcher, Hay and Straw Dealer, along with fisherman, butcher, basket maker, fruit grower, market gardener, and even a watchmaker! Many of these jobs helped to make the parishes self- sufficient.

One notable listed occupation was that of Alfred Youngs who was listed as a steam threshing machine owner in the 1890s as well as a pork butcher.

Robert Gedge had another interesting occupation as a plumber, glazier and painter for many years

# THE HALVERGATE FLEET

The Halvergate Fleet is a relict natural saltwater creek running from Halvergate through the marshes to Breydon Water. It is about 4 miles long. The source of the Fleet is not far from the Red Lion Public House on Marsh Road in Halvergate .

Land submergence and elevation thousands of years ago altered the coastline of East Anglia and the area now occupied by the marshes of the lower Bure, Yare and Waveney were once part of a shallow bay or estuary. The gradual elevation of the land combined with the formation of a sandbank at what has become Great Yarmouth and the silting up of the estuary has created the marshlands. Embankment of the rivers probably began around the twelfth century and helped in the reclamation of the marshland. In the thirteenth century the sea level was about thirteen feet lower than it is today!

As the silting of the estuary occurred natural creeks and rivulets were formed which drained away the salt waters at low tide. The Halvergate Fleet is the longest one of the many naturally formed creeks to be found across the marshlands.

As the marshland was reclaimed from the estuary it was allocated to existing parishes. The marshes bordering Halvergate were allocated to distant parishes and so we had a detached South Walsham, a detached Acle, a detached Postwick, a detached Burlingham and several others detached parishes scattered across the marshes.

To assist in draining the marshes, other dykes and smaller drains were cut across the marshes and a number of drainage mills were built close to the Halvergate Fleet to drain water from the man-made dykes into the Fleet and then into Breydon Water. About 18 miles of main drains across the marshes drain into the Fleet. A sluice gate was also constructed at the end of the Fleet at Breydon Water to control the draining of the Fleet water into Breydon and to prevent the tidal waters entering the Fleet dyke. Other drainage mills across these detached marshes drained into other dykes and into the River Bure or the River Yare.

Marsh-houses were also constructed close to most of the mills. The houses were occupied by the marshmen, who operated the mills, and their families. The marshmen did much more than operate the drainage mills. They were also responsible for tending the cattle, clearing the dykes and drains, repairing the fences, mowing thistles and generally looking after the marshland. A marshman's wage was often low and most of them supplemented their income by shooting wildfowl and game, of which there was once plenty on the marshes, and by keeping chickens, geese and their own cows.

Most mills and marsh houses were remote from the village centres and the embanked Fleet wall was probably the main track between Halvergate and Great Yarmouth for many centuries. The following section provides some information about the many drainage mills to be found within the boundaries of the current Halvergate parish. Some of these mills were in detached parts of other parishes.

# HALVERGATE DRAINAGE MILLS AND PUMPS

## STRACEY ARMS MILL TG442090

**STRACEY ARMS MILL** lies to the south of the River Bure and was in the old Tunstall parish. This was often called **ARNUP'S MILL** since it was worked by several members of the Arnup family.

A mill was marked here on the 1884 OS map as a 'draining pump'. On the 1826 map a mill was shown here as **TUNSTALL MILL**, and on Faden's map it was marked as 'Drain W Mill'.

On the Tithe Map, circa 1840, a mill was marked on area 147, which was listed as

the Mill Marsh. It was owned by Edward Stracey and occupied by Christmas Francis, who was at the Stracey Arms public house according to the Tithe Apportionment. The adjacent building on area 148 was listed as 'Cottage & Garden' and was listed as owned and occupied by Edward Stracey. This was the dwelling where many of the subsequent marshmen lived.

This mill is now owned by Norfolk County Council and looked after by Norfolk Windmills Trust. It was previously owned by the Stracey family, hence the name, and was gifted to the council by Lady Stracey in 1965.

The mill marked here on the early maps would have been a primitive mill.

The present mill is a red brick tower, three storeys high, and about 36 feet to the top of the tower. The inside diameter at the base is 10 ft 6 in and at the top of the brick work it is 6 ft 9 inches in diameter. It is said to have been built, or rebuilt, in 1883 by Richard Barnes, of Gt Yarmouth, on 40 foot piles topped with a raft of pitchpine. At that time it was a patent sail mill and drove a scoopwheel. A turbine pump was installed later by Smithdales of Acle in 1912.

During WWII the mill was used as a pillbox by the home guard.

A 20hp electric pump was built here in about 1942 and took over from the mill. It could lift 28 tons per minute.

Smithdales of Acle did some restoration work on the mill in 1961 and more restoration work has continued under the guidance of the Norfolk Windmills Trust. John Lawn did some work on the mill for the Norfolk Windmills Trust.

The sails turned clockwise. There is one door, 2 windows on the first floor and 2 windows on the top floor. The external turbine pump and the machinery inside the mill still exist.

The mill house nearby was where the millman or marshman lived. Some of the occupants were:

1841, 1851,1861, 1871 census returns: William Arnup .

1881, 1891, 1901, 1911 census returns: George Arnup.

1916 & 1925 Kelly's Directories: George Arnup, marshman.

1937 Kelly's Directory: Leonard Arnup, marshman.

Later Fred Mutton was the marshman here during the 1940s 50s & 60s.

'Paddy' Walker lived in the mill house in the 1970s and his wife looked after the mill which was open to the public. The mill house incorporates a small shop and offers provisions for boating holiday-makers. The mill house and shop are currently up for sale

## YOUNGS MILL TG432096

A 'drainage pump' was shown on the south side of the Tunstall Dyke, where the dyke enters the Bure, on the OS maps of circa 1884, 1907 and 1951.

A mill was also shown here on the Tunstall Tithe Map, circa 1840, on the area numbered 137. It was owned and occupied at that time by Isaac Everit. The adjacent area 136, was shown as 'house and yards' and was occupied then by John Howell and owned by Isaac Everit.

John Howell was probably responsible for operating the mill here and was listed in the 1851 and 1861 census. Others that may have lived here are: 1871 and 1881 Census: either William Rumbold or Robert Turner 1891 Census: Scurrell Youngs, 1925, 1933, 1937 directories: George Youngs. George Youngs was still living here as a marshman in the 1940s.

The last mill here was a cloth sailed tower mill believed to have been built in 1818. The mill was shown on Bryant's map of 1826 as '**Tunstall Mill'**. Faden's Map of 1797 also shows an earlier mill here.

70

The level here was sometimes referred to as Gowing's Level.

The old mill house was pulled down and a new dwelling has been erected on the site.

Nearby an electric PUMPING STATION is shown on the 1996 map where Tunstall Dyke meets the river.

## SIX MILE HOUSE DRAINAGE MILL TG461098

**SIX MILE HOUSE DRAINAGE MILL** is shown on the 1996 OS map on the south side of the River Bure. It is a grade 2 listed building. This area was once the detached part of Cantley parish.

A mill was marked here on all maps from 1797, and was marked as 'Drain W Mill' on Faden's 1797 map, as **'CANTLEY MILL'** on Bryant's 1826 map, and as a 'draining pump' in 1884. It has been called by several other names including **BLAKE'S MILL** and **LAKE'S MILL** and **WLLIAM PERRY'S MILL**. On the Cantley Tithe Map & Apportionment, circa 1840, area 233 is marked as 'Mill, House & Yards etc' and is owned by Mrs Shuckford and occupied by Isaac Gown jnr.

The present mill is a tarred redbrick tower mill, four storeys high with an external scoopwheel. The tower has a lean and corrugated sheeting is on the top. It is a grade 2 listed building. This last mill is believed to have been built in the 1870s and last worked in the mid 1940s.

The building firm of R.G. Carter owned the mill, house and several acres here at one time and they sold it in about 1976. It is now privately owned. There is now a pump house nearby.

Some of the marshmen here from the Cantley census returns were: 1851 & 1861 census returns: Isaac Gowen, 1871, 1881 & 1891census returns: George Thaxter, 1901 Frederick Bailey, 1911 James David Hewitt. Mr Robert Lake was the marshman in the 1930s and 1940s.

71

## TUNSTALL DYKE DRAINAGE MILL TG422092

Marked on the 1826 and all subsequent maps it lies on the north side if the dyke in the old parish of Tunstall. No mill was marked here on the 1797 map.

On the Tithe Map this was area 59 marked as 'Mill & Yard', owned by Stephen Bailey and occupied by James Skinner.

A mill is marked here on the 1996 OS Map as **'Tunstall Dyke Drainage Mill'**. This is a grade 2 listed building and was a 4 storey brick tower mill and had an external scoopwheel of 13 ft 4 inch diameter. The tower is about 24 ft to the curb and the external diameter at the base is about 16ft. Walls are 2 ft thick at the base of the tower. There are 2 doors and a ground floor window, 2 windows on the first floor and a further window at second floor level.

A. C. Smith writing in 1990 said that it was in a very derelict state but had an iron rack on top and an iron pit wheel of 7 ft diameter, its shaft going to the external scoop wheel.

## TUNSTALL SMOCK DRAINAGE MILL TG423092

This is marked on the 1996 OS map. This was also shown on the 1951 OS map and the 1907 OS map as a 'drainage pump'. This is in the old parish of Tunstall and is located on the south east side of Tunstall Dyke.

On the OS map of circa 1884 the mill was **not** shown here but another 'drainage pump' was shown closer to the Tunstall Staithe at about TG421091.

On the earlier

Tunstall Tithe Map and on Bryant's map of 1826 a mill was again marked at TG423092. A 'Drain W Mill' was also marked near here on Faden's map of 1797, but the exact location is not clear.

On the Tithe Map area 91 was marked as 'Mill & Yard', the owner was Andrew Fountaine and the occupier listed as Richard Gillett. The early mill at TG 423092 must have become obsolete and another 'pump' was built at TG421091 near the staithe sometime before the 1880s, and then a further mill was built on, or near, the original site around the turn of the century.

According to AC Smith writing in 1989 the smock mill here was derelict and was reduced to about 12 ft in height. It was octagonal in shape with horizontal boards and had a boarded shed attached. He says it contained no machinery at that time, but had once had an internal turbine pump.

It is truncated to 2 storeys and about 2/3rds of its original height and was given a sloping corrugated iron roof in 1994.

In about 1941 an electric pump was installed nearby and this could pump up to 25 tons of water per minute.

## KEY'S MILL TG462085

This mill last worked in the mid 1940s and is located in the old Acle Detached Parish.

Sometimes called the **'Black Mill'** or **'Kerrison's Mill'**, lying on Kerrison's Level, this mill is located on the south side of the Acle New Road and the railway line. It pumped water into a dyke which runs into the River Bure. It is a grade 2 listed building and is currently looked after by the Norfolk Windmills Trust and was leased for 99 years to the Norfolk County Council in 1982.

No mill was shown here on the 1797 map or the 1799 Acle Enclosure map, but a mill was shown on Bryant's map and all subsequent maps. Bryant's 1826 map shows this as **'Acle Mill'**

On the Acle Tithe Map of 1838 a mill was marked on area 708 and a house on area 707. The owner and occupier of the house and mill was given as Mathias Harrison.

This is a redbrick tower mill, tarred black, four storeys high and is about 32 ft high to the curb. It has a window on the second floor and another on the top floor. The inside diameter at the base is about 12 ft 9 inches, and the wall thickness is 18 inches. Six metal bands encircle the tower and the barter changes at the top suggesting it was 'hained' at some time. It also has two metal tie-rods. It has a white boat shaped cap with petticoat, but no sails or stocks. The external scoopwheel is about 17 ft 3 inches in diameter.

The mill was attended to for many years by the Bailey family who lived in the nearby farmhouse. From the censuses we find the following:
1861& 1881 census returns: Samuel Bailey, 1891: Frederick Bailey, 1901 & 1911 census: William Bailey.

In March 1938 the mill, marshman's house and 261 acres of Kerrison's Level was put up for sale. The mill was in working order and drained about 380 acres; the mill rents amounting to £25-15s-6d. The marshman was W. Bailey. (ref NRO/BR143/113).
In 1948 Mrs Bailey was given as the marshman (NRO/BR143/114).

In 1950 Kerison's Level was sold again by direction of G.C. Hughes. The level was 260 acres and included the old now disused mill and the marshman's house. The sitting tenant in the house was marshman W. Parker whose annual rent was £10. The house is brick built, and at that time was part tiled and part thatched.

From 1952 the marshman on Kerrison's Level living at 'Black Mill Farm' was W. R. Mallett. The Hon Major H.R. Broughton was the owner of Kerrison's Level in 1960 (NRO/BR143/115).

## HALVERGATE STEAM MILL

This was located on Marsh Road Halvergate at about TG462069.
This was marked on the 1883 OS map as '**Corn Mill and Draining Pump**'.
It is believed to have been a steam mill driving a paddle wheel, built in the 1860s for draining the Hall level into the Halvergate Fleet. It was also used for milling cake. It was a red brick building with a slate roof.
Mr Thomas Kidner Esq. of Halvergate Hall owned the steam mill in the early 1900s, and Myrus Sutton acquired it when he took over Halvergate Hall.

There was a wooden house near to the steam mill, where Marsh Road, Branch Road and Stone Road meet and this was referred to as Wooden Hut Corner. This wooden house was occupied for some time by the Mallet family.
After a wide dyke was made from the Engine Carr to Stone's Mill the SteamMmill was no longer required, and the steam mill stopped working in the 1920's.
The last known operator was 'Chummy' Alfred Mallett who lived in the The City. The boiler was removed in the early 1930s and the building was finally demolished in the early 1950s. In the Halvergate censuses we find the following entries:

74

1871 & 1881: Alfred Mallet, Engine driver, 1891: Alfred Mallet, Steam Engine Driver (son of above Alfred)

**Wooden House at Wooden Hut Corner at the junction of Marsh Road, Branch Road and Stone Road. Supplied by Joy Brock.**

**Wooden Hut. This may be members of Mallett Family living here.**

## CARTER'S MILL. TG441058

Fred Carter in 1952

This was also known as **STONE'S MILL.**
It stands on Baker's level, and was first shown on
Faden's map of 1797. It was also shown on
Bryant's map as the '**Halvergate Mill**', and was
also shown on the 1839 Halvergate Tithe Award
map. In 1842 the land where this mill stood
belonged to a Maria Nesbitt and was occupied, or
worked, by Ben Howard according to the Tithe
Apportionment of that date. Ben Howard was
living at the Manor House, according to the 1841 census.

The mill was later owned by Myrus Sutton for many years, and was
operated by Leonard Carter until he died in 1918, then by Wes Stone, and later by
Fred Carter, nicknamed 'Orkshire'. Fred was one of Leonard Carter's sons.

The mill was 3 storeys high and may have been built, or rebuilt, by Barnes
of Yarmouth but had machinery from an earlier mill. It drove an external
scoopwheel. It was a Brick tower with patent sails but may have previously been
cloth-sailed. The sails turned anti-clockwise with 48 shutters per sail. It had an 8
bladed fantail and a boat-shaped cap with no gallery. The cogs were made with
apple-wood and needed regular replacement, and the other internal wooden parts
were made from ash and pine. The brass ends required frequent greasing as it got
very hot. The mill was last operated in 1948 by Fred Carter, and the mill was
demolished in the early 1950s.

## MUTTON'S MILL TG442064

This was also known as **MANOR HOUSE MILL**.

Bryant's Map of 1826 shows '**Fellows Farm & Mill**' at this approximate location, but another mill had existed nearby in 1769, and was also shown on a map of 1803. This earlier mill was probably demolished sometime in the 1820's or 1830's when it was replaced by a mill some 200m to the SW.

The name 'Fellows' above must refer to the family of Robert Fellowes Esq. of Shotesham Park who was listed in White's and in Kelly's directories as Lord of the Manor and was a major landowner in Halvergate. He owned the land and mill in the 1840s at the time of the Tithe Apportionment.

The mill stands on what was once called the Frothelmes Level and was a black tarred red brick tower with 4 patent sails, which turned anti-clockwise. The sails were double shuttered with 8 bays, with 3 shutters each, giving 48 per sail. It had a 6 bladed fantail and a boat-shaped cap.

It is 4 storeys high, with a height of about 40 ft to the curb. The base diameter is 24 ft, and the curb diameter 14 ft. It had an internal scoop wheel, 15.5 feet in diamcter, with 18 inch wide paddles.

It is possible that it was built or rebuilt built by Stolworthy of Yarmouth.

It was last worked in about 1947 by Fred Mutton and was derelict for several years with 4 sails.

The mill was at one time owned by Lady Stracey until it was sold off.

Paul Reynolds and David High took the mill over in 1974. Some repairs were done in 1976, and a new cap and fantail was fitted in 1984, and one set of sails was fitted in 1998.

Some of the marshmen at the nearby Manor Farm House who operated the mill include John Howard listed in 1841, Benjamin Howard from 1851 to 1881, James Mutton 1891, Frederick Howard Mutton, Fred Mutton jnr.

## MY FATHER FRED MUTTON by URSULA BREWER

Fred was born in 1923 in a small farmhouse by the river near Acle; this house no longer exists but I believe there is still a building there.

Dad was one of 10 children, being one of two boys with the rest girls. He went to school in Acle, usually setting off with good intentions to go, but it would not be long before his mother would see a small figure coming back home as his delight was to help his father on the marshes. He would only have been about five years old!

The marshes became his life, being born into five generations of marshmen he knew how to make a living from them, the changing seasons providing a variety of jobs.

In the 1940s grandfather Mutton took over as marshman with the Stracey Arms Mill, and Manor Farm was succeeded there by my father in about 1943, at the age of twenty. Manor Farm then was essentially a purpose built Dairy Farm, with cowsheds and a dairy attached to the house. There was a much older farm on this site but it was demolished and the present house built in its place.

The milk had to be transported across the marshes and rutted track-way by horse and cart for collection at the nearest roadside.

Dad met and married Joan in 1947 and they settled at Manor Farm. Because the Halvergate grass was rich, farmers would send cattle for summer grazing, Dad's job then was to count them daily and check their well-being. For this he would be paid at the end of the year so money would have to be spread over many months. Extra money earned would come from dyke dredging, thistle mowing and other manual work all done by hand.

I came along in 1948 and all my early years were spent growing up at Manor Farm, then the marshes were teeming with cattle, cattle floats were everywhere, loading up and bringing more cattle to the lush marshes. Dad a reputation for being a "quick walker", he could cover marshland at speed which was legendry. Roger Clarke would always remark on this, probably after trailing behind Dad to tend some sick animal.

The mill, aptly named Muttons Mill, is only a short distance from Manor Farm. Dad regularly tended to the water levels and general maintenance of the mill. It was built by ancestor James Mutton together with William Hewitt and Hindle of Reedham.

James was a master bricklayer and built many of the drainage mills in the nineteenth century. His initials are clearly carved in a mill brick, "J.M. 1909."

Things changed as times moved on, the isolation of Manor Farm became something my mother could no longer bear and in the early sixties they moved into Halvergate village. Dad did not give up the marshes but "commuted" daily, the horse being replaced by a car. Although he continued to keep cattle, the living gained from such a life dwindled and he found work elsewhere.

My father never lost his love of the marshes, or his delight in a good yarn with friends. He always lived in sight of his beloved marshes and Muttons Mill. Sadly we lost him in 2007, but I feel sure his spirit is roaming Halvergate marshes happy and contented!

MANOR FARM HOUSE 1970

**Fred Mutton**

## HIGH'S MILL TG457072

Located in Halvergate Parish on the Fleet Dyke, the mill has been known by many other names over the years: **COTMAN'S MILL, LUBBOCK'S MILL, GILBERT'S MILL, HARDEN'S MILL** and even as **Carter's Mill.**

Bryant's 1826 map of Norfolk shows at this approximate location a mill, named as '**Halvergate Mill**', and a nearby building, probably the marsh farmhouse, labelled as 'Hewetts'. A mill and marsh house were also shown hereabouts on the earlier 1797 Faden's map.

This mill and the house were on Cotman's level, hence the name Cotman's mill.

The mill was originally built in the 18th century. It was a small tarred red brick 2 storey tower mill with a boat-shaped cap and common sails which turned clockwise into the wind. It had an internal fireplace and only one window. It had no fantail but instead a tail-pole, winch and chains for turning the sails into the wind. It drained about 200 acres and had a 12 ft diameter external scoop wheel.

It had canvas cloth sails and Bertie High said only 2 sails were issued when he was there, but he made 2 more from sacking. When the strength of the wind changed the sail cloths would have to be adjusted and if the wind direction changed the cap had to be winched into the wind. The mill was last worked by Len Carter in 1948. In 1980 the mill was re-tarred and it now has a temporary aluminium cap. The mill is now looked after by the Norfolk Windmills Trust

**Wes Tooley & Bertie High.**

The **Marsh house** TG457070 was probably built in the early 1700's, and was of brick and tiles. The last occupant at the marsh house was Len Carter, who moved in to the marsh house in 1945. The house was eventually demolished by Mr Lanham in about 1965 or 1966. Bertie High and his family occupied the house from 1943 to 1945. Bertie's father James Thomas High was the official marshman who lived here from 1900 to 1943. He and his sons operated the mill.

Other occupants from earlier census returns include: Ben Banham in 1891, Last Banham in 1881 & 1871, either George Thaxter or Robert Turner in 1861, and Samuel Agus in 1851. The 1842 Tithe Apportionment lists Henry Sharman as occupant.

## HOWARD'S MILL TG463073

This was located on the Halvergate Fleet on the South Walsham (St. Lawrence) Detached Parish, South Walsham Marshes. This became part of Halvergate parish in 1935. It has also been known in the past as **SOUTH WALSHAM MILL**.

A mill was marked on Faden's map of 1797, and Bryant's map of 1826 shows a 'South Walsham' mill at this approximate.

The present mill was probably a rebuild, done around 1880. The tower predates the iron machinery by about 40 years, so the tower may have been built about 1840.

At ground level rough brickwork of the previous tower can be seen and in places the present brickwork does not align with the old footings. The mill is a tarred Red Brick Tower, 3 storeys high, about 30 ft to the curb, with 2 doors and 2 windows on each upper level. It had 4 patent sails, an 8-bladed fantail and Norfolk boat-shaped cap. Each sail had 8 bays, double shuttered, with 3 vanes each, giving 48 vanes per sail. The sails were about 25feet long and 7 ft 6inches wide. It had a 16 feet scoop-wheel, with the inscription Smihdale & Sons on the scoop-wheel gate. The brick culvert was about 8 inches wide and was rebuilt in the 1930's. The cap, fly-frame and sails were by W.T. England. The main machinery was by Robert Barnes of Southtown about 1880. Some iron floor supports bear the name W. T. England Yarmouth 1911. The following initials were found on the woodwork: AJT 1904 (A.J.Thrower), JWT, AK England, WA England 1924, R Want 1934, on the sluicegate: 'Smithdale', and on the upright shaft 'H.H. R.B. W.F.1898'.

The mill was last worked in 1947 using only 2 sails, after 2 of the sails were taken down and possibly used elsewhere. Ben Howard was the last marshman to work the mill. It remained derelict for several years.

The mill, and marshes, was owned by Lady Stracey, and later the mill was bought by Richard Seago in 1978 from Fairhaven Estates. Richard Seago began repairing the mill with the help of grants from the Broads Authority.
The cap was blown off in Jan 1978 and Seago put a temporary corrugated metal sheet roof on top. Repairs to the mill were carried out during the 1980's and a new cap and fantail were fitted on 29th August 1989. Richard Seago put the mill up for sale in April 2001 with a price tag of £32,000.

The Marsh House stands to the east of the mill at about TG464072.
It is thought to have been built in the seventeenth century and had three bedrooms. It was shown on the 1826 map as 'Hewetts'. It is now known as 'Marsh Farm, Berney Arms'. It is built of brick with a thatched roof. It now has a private cesspit, it's own electricity generator and water is obtained from a spring.
Some marshman occupants of the house include Edward Hewitt in 1841 – 1861, John Howard 1871 – 1891, Ben Howard 1901 - 1940s, Billy Lacey 1950s – 1963. The house was sold in 1964 as a private residence.

## GOFFIN'S MILL, TG464070.

Located in Halvergate Parishon the Fleet Dyke, This mill was also known as MINISTER'S MILL, WALPOLE'S MILL and sometimes as HEWITT'S MILL after the owners and/or marshman who lived in the nearby marsh house and worked the mill.

A mill was marked on Faden's map, 1797, at this location, and a mill, not named, was shown at this approximate location on Bryant's map of 1826. Also a mill was marked on the HalvergateTithe map at this location. It is probable that the mill was rebuilt or altered over the years. The last structure standing was a typical brick tower mill with 4 patent sails, each with 9 bays, double-shuttered, 3 per bay, giving 54 shutters per sail. It had a fantail with 8 blades, and a boat-shaped cap and drove an external scoopwheel. It is believed to have been built or rebuilt by Stolworthy.
The mill was last worked by Fred Hewitt, in about 1948, and it was demolished in the 1950's..

In 1840s Tithe Apportionment the mill and landowner was Sir Edward Walpole Esq. It was later owned by Myrus Sutton.

The Marsh House stands a few yards to the east of the mill at about TG465070. It is believed to be late seventeenth century built. It was shown on Bryant's map as Walpole's Farm in 1826, and was shown on the Halvergate Tithe map. It still exists and is now known as Fleet Farm, Berney Arms. Fred Nichols was last marshman at the house. The house remained empty for a while after he left in 1966 but was then acquired by Mr F. Futter. Some earlier occupants include: Henry Everson in the 1950s, Fred Hewitt in the 1930-40s, James Goffin in the1920s, James Brown in 1911, and James Minister 1841 – 1891 census returns.

**Fred and Hannah Hewitt at the marsh house next to Goffin's Mill in the 1940s.**

**Halvergate Village Celebrations for the postponed 1937 Coronation.**
**Top: Fred Lake with Trixie.**
**Bottom: From the left: Amy Youngs, Brenda Key, Doris Youngs, and Dorothy Tovell.**
**Photographs from Joy Brock.**

84

# DESMOND SHARMAN REMEMBERS

I was born 14<sup>th</sup> December 1925 at Hall Cottage and moved to No. 5 Mill Road in 1928. This was a newly built house and I lived there for twenty years till I got married. Many children lived on Mill Road and football and cricket was played on the road. There were no cars to worry about in those days.

In the 1930s all the gardens were well looked after. Water was drawn from a well situated between numbers 8 and 9 and this served all twelve houses.

I went to Halvergate primary school from the age of 5. The head teacher was Miss Wheeler. Other teachers included Mrs Foster and Miss Mary Beck. There were various sports to be played and the education was mainly reading, writing, arithmetic and religious education. I did not like school from day one; to me it was very boring. The school dentist came with a caravan. At eleven years of age I went to Freethorpe School where the main teachers were Mr Rogers and Mrs Girdlestone. Mrs Clark was the dinner lady and also taught cooking, while Mr Bacon was the school carpenter. I left school at 14 in 1939 and in January 1940 I took a job at British Sugar Corporation as a sugar packer and then running a packing machine. When I was 16 all the boys working there had to leave to make way for jobs for the woman and as I was too young for the forces I looked for another job and found one at the farm of Mr R. J. More, in Tunstall. Denis Willimott was the head cowman on More's farm, other cowmen were Albert Tovell, Ronnie Mallett and Billy Rowland.

Shops I remember in the village include: The post office, run by Eddie Youngs and his wife, who took over from Frank Youngs; Walter Jermy had a grocery and butchers shop on Marsh Road near the Red Lion; Mr & Mrs Rowland had a grocery shop on Squires Road where they also had a drapery and bicycle shop selling 'Runwell Cycles'. It was open till ten o'clock at night.

On Wednesdays and Saturdays Woolsey coaches ran from Halvergate to Great Yarmouth. In later years, Lake coaches took on this job.

The earliest doctor's surgery I recall was on Squires Road at Mrs Muttons place; the doctors were Blake and Fletcher.

There were three bakers that delivered around the village: Grays, Purdys, and Dick Woodcock who was the rounds-man delivering bread from the local mill / bakery run by Mr Wright. Our milk was delivered from the Post Office as Eddie

Youngs had his own herd of cows. I remember that the Red Lion pub was run by Jim and Reene Bond.

Mill Road was like a small community on its own and we would have our own large bonfire on November 5th and have a get together.

I went to Sunday School at the Wickhampton Chapel where the superintendant was Fred Howard. Another teacher there was Mrs Best. On Wednesday evenings in the summer we would have a short service followed by games and entertainment. At the end Mrs Best would throw monkey nuts into the road for us children to gather. There was outings arranged by the Wickhampton Chapel and the Anniversaries were held every year and were well attended with many people standing on the road outside.

Morning, afternoon and evening services were held and many recitations said by the children. Collections were taken to give the children outings at Gorleston and Great Yarmouth and meals were provided. An annual camp meeting was also held on the Lawn in June or July and these were well attended.

Mr Benjamin Wright owned the mill and ground flour and made bread. He also owned a piece of land and grew vegetables and sugar beet. The mill burnt down in about 1935, I remember seeing it on fire, the sails going around alight.

**1935
Silver Jubilee**

The Silver Jubilee of King George V and Queen Mary, May 4th 1935, was a big occasion. Everyone was dressed up and a big carnival was held with a parade around the village. Albert Bradshaw played a trumpet as we marched around the village. I was dressed as a wounded soldier, my cousin Stella was as a nurse, and my sister rode a big black horse belonging to Mr W. Lake. She carried a white star to represent peace. The parade was followed by sports on the Lawn on Wickhampton Road and then a big sit-down meal at the Dutch Barn on Tunstall Road. A commemorative cup and saucer was given to all the children to mark the occasion.

I was in the Homeguard as a messenger at the age of 15 and I had to bike to Bradistone to take messages. Later I was enrolled as a member of the Freethorpe patrol. During night duty we used the coach house at Halvergate. I remember one night on exercises when we had to cross all the marshes to take the Reedham Swing Bridge, and in the morning I had to go to work!

When I lived at Mill Road during the war years I remember a plane coming down on the Halvergate or Wickhampton marshes. There was also a plane come down one morning at about six o'clock on Mr More's land in Tunstall. I can remember that there was a big naval gun on the Reedham Road near the plantation.

I played football for Halvergate till I was 52 years of age and I got involved as a manager for 11 years.

I worked for R. J. More of Tunstall, from the age of 16 up until 1959, when Mr More died. I had a very enjoyable time working there. I had many jobs there; starting very early in the morning my first job was to collect the milk by pony and cart which was located at Low Farm Road. The work there was piece work so I earned good money. There were about 33 men working on the farm. Mr More grew currants on many acres and picking time was busy during July and August. There would be as many as 200 pickers employed being paid at ten pence a stone. The pickers took their pails of currents to be weighed and given a ticket at the end of the day. The tickets would be handed in at the farm at the end of the season and the pickers were then paid. About 120 tons would be picked during a season and the currents went to Hartley Jam Factory. After the War Pheasant Shoots were held on More's and I went 'brushing'. Some of those attending the shoot were Dr Francis, John Francis Arthur Shearing and the Colonel. At lunch break Mrs Newson provided us with baked potatoes, cheese and onions and a stone jar of beer in the stables.

After Mr More died I had to find other employment outside of the villages and had a job at Birds Eye for a time and again went back to British Sugar Corporation and later had a security job.

I was married in 1945 to Lucy and we had seven children. My wife was a dinner lady and care taker for many years at the Halvergate primary school till it closed in 1988. All our children went to Halvergate School and they attended the Halvergate chapel anniversaries which were held in Maurice Sutton's barn in Wickhampton. The house on Church Avenue where we lived had electric and running water when we moved in. I have now lived in Halvergate all my life and cannot think of a better place to have lived.

## HALVERGATE FOOTBALL CLUB BY DESMOND H SHARMAN, FORMER CLUB CHAIRMAN.

The club was founded in the 1920s.
First Played on land owned by Mr Myrus Sutton and known locally as 'The Lawn' situated on Wickhampton Road. They continued to play home matches there until April 1979 when the property was bought by Mr Robert Chase.

From 1920 until 1932 Halvergate F.C. played in the Reedham & District League of which they were Champions in 1926-27. Joined the Yarmouth &

District League in 1932 winning the 2<sup>nd</sup> Division and getting promoted to the 1st Division where they stayed until the big move to the Anglia Combination 1992.

The Reserve Team played in the Yarmouth & District League Division 3 which they were Champions of in year 1946-47, also winners of the Blofield District League.

A Minor Team was founded in 1946-47 and ran until 1953. Home matches for the Minors were on a meadow owned by Mr Robert Moore on Tunstall Road. The changing room was a cart shed, as was the same for many more village teams. The Minors were Losing Finalists in the Minor Cup 1951-52.
This land is now a Housing Estate joining together the Villages of Halvergate and Tunstall.

The First Teams achievements on record includes:-
Runners-Up - Wiltshire Cup - 1947-48
Winners - Wiltshire Cup - 1948-49

**Holmes Cup Winners 1948-49.Back Row: Willimont, Mallett, Howard, Long, Yaxley, Carter
Front Row: Carter, Lake, Mallett, Barrett, Harper**

Winners - Holmes Cup - 1948-49
Runners-Up - League Division I - 1952-53
Also won Wiltshire Cup again & Runners-Up in League Cup (Holmes Cup renamed) in 1952-53.

After the War ended in 1945, Charity Matches were played among the local teams. These matches were played at the end of the season on a knock-out basis and were difficult to fit in if you were successful.

There was the Freethorpe Charity Cup, Acle Charity Cup, Blofield Charity Cup, Beighton Charity Cup, Reedham Charity Cup, Halvergate Charity

88

Cup, and the Fishley Cup for the Reserve Teams. The Cup Owners invited the local Clubs to enter these matches. These matches were very keenly played after a days work, and most of the village people turned up to watch their team, sometimes as many as 100.

On one occasion Halvergate had to play Reedham in two Cup Finals and Acle in another on the last day of the season. These tournaments went on until the 1970's.

In 1975 a Committee was formed to discuss the purchase of 5 acres of land from the late Mr Myruss Sutton's executors situated next to the old ground. The purchase was completed and came to use in 1981. Meanwhile the club had been playing home matches at Cantley.

A Clubhouse was erected near to Wickhampton Road and 2 portacabins were purchased from Norwich City F. C. for use as dressing rooms with showers added. The late 70's and early 80's was a very hard time for the club, mainly due to the unavailability of players, but managed to carry on running 2 teams.

During the late 80's things improved, several younger local players came through the system, and their first taste of success was winning Division 1 of the Yarmouth League and being Champions for the first in the clubs history. Next was my proudest moment as the club Chairman when we reached the Final of the Norfolk Junior Cup and played at the Norwich City Ground at Carrow Road. We finished as Runners-Up after a Replay.

**Boys Five-a-side team.**

A very big move was made by joining the Anglia Combination Division 4. After winning that league we were on our way again to reach the heights and after several good seasons were promoted to the lst Division and the taste of senior football after 5 years.

Sunday Football was introduced in 1983 winning Division 4 and 3, Runners-Up Division 2 and our highest position 3$^{rd}$ of Division 1, Winners of Knock-Out Cup the final being played at Emerald Park - A very good 13 years!

The Club folded in 2007-08.

**Winners of Division III Yarmouth League 1947-48**

JOHN WILLIMOTT, JIM TOVELL, ROYSTON MALLETT, BLIMEY, COSTESSEY, CHARLIE CARTER, WILF LAKE, RONNIE LONG, DENNIS YAXLEY, SID SPRINGALL, DENNIS HOWARD

**Wiltshire Cup Winners 1952-53.**
Back Row from left: Stan Ellis, J Tovell, Billy Willimott, R. Barrett, R.Long, D. Yaxley, J. Willimott, R Sevill, Mr R.J.More.
Front Row: R Carter, W.Lake, C. Mallett, R. Mallett, F. Harper, C. Carter.

**1950 Minor Team**

**1927 Halvergate Football Team; From the back left: Frank Carter, Wilf Mallett, Ben Beck, Dan Fransham, Billy Lawn. Middle row: Dick Woodcock, George Foster, Benny Wright, Ernest 'Boyse' Knights, Cyrus Mallett. Front: Joe Starkins, Reg 'Rice Pie' Carter, and Bob 'Teaser' Carter. Photo supplied by Heather Wright**.

## BOWLS CLUB.

A Bowls Club was formed in 1921/22 and played on the green at the Vicarage. Later they club played by the Church until Mr R. J. More provided a field, Top Green on Squires Road. This was a men only club till 1945 when the club allowed female members.

## HAPPY CIRCLE

This was formed in 1950 and arranged social gatherings and outings for the older people of the village, and meetings at the village hall. The Happy Circle continues to thrive to this day.

**Happy Circle gathering. Supplied by Des Sharman**

## HALVERGATE PLAYING FIELD

This is located on the west side of Wickhampton Road and is a 5.5 acre field which has two football pitches, a children's play area, a floodlit games area and a licensed clubhouse / pavilion. The clubhouse was built, and ready for use, by 1983. The Halvergate Playing Field Association was formed in 1976 and is a registered charity run by local volunteers. The Halvergate football and cricket teams play their home games here.

## CAROL HANNANT RECALLS

Years of effort and dedicated hard work by all the Community made a dream come true for devout sports enthusiast, Mr. Ben Beck as he officially opened the new Halvergate Playing Field in June 1983. Mr. Beck had been involved with the Halvergate Football and Cricket Clubs all his life and quoted that he had always dreamed of the Village owning its own Playing Field, especially after losing the use of a courtesy field on the Lawn at Halvergate Hall, making the clubs exiles to the Village for a number of years, forcing them to play Football and Cricket on other grounds further afield.

This great achievement became a reality after a piece of land had been purchased from a local landowner and slowly transformed into a Village Playing Field complete with a Clubhouse and changing facilities. This had been made possible by a Committee of dedicated Villagers who raised money through Fetes, Coffee Mornings, Village Bonfires, Car Rallies, Sponsored Walks, etc. etc.

The fund raising didn't stop there and since that day thousands of pounds has been raised to add new features to the facility including an extension and complete exterior and interior renovation of the Clubhouse, a floodlit multi-use games area, a regenerated Children's Play area and improvements to the playing surfaces.

The Field has now been registered with the Fields in Trust as a Queen Elizabeth II playing field and protected as green space for many generations to come.

**Pictured is Mr. Ben Beck with Committee Members. Back row left to right: Janet Baxter, Dawn Tovell, Carol Hannant, Paul Pitchers, David Hannant, Tony Baxter, and Royston Mallett. Front Row: Jackie Broom and Amy Youngs. Supplied by Carol Hannant.**

## BETTY TORTICE REMEMBERS

I got involved with the Halvergate Playing Field when I became friends with Marjorie Mallett. Halvergate had Saturday and Sunday football teams: Marjorie and I used to make cups of tea and sausage rolls for the players and spectators. I also helped with refreshments for the Saturday team.

Many local people have various parties and wedding receptions at the clubhouse. We have Easter and Christmas "all prize" bingos, Easter egg hunts for the children, Halloween Parties and a Christmas Extravaganzas each year at the playing field clubhouse. Here I always have my fete to raise funds for the East Coast Truckers on the first Sunday in June each year.

We held our Golden Jubilee and Diamond Jubilee celebrations at the playing field.

**Queen Elizabeth's Golden Jubilee celebrations. Left to right: Kirsty Handford (attendant), Erin Kelf (Queen) and Melissa Hannant (attendant). Supplied by Betty Tortice**

## MEMORIES OF HALVERGATE CRICKET CLUB BY EDWIN YOUNGS.

My first memories of Halvergate Cricket Club stem from a diary which my late Aunt Amy Youngs had kept many years ago when Halvergate used to play in the old Blofield and District League, going back to the late 1800's. Local teams, such as Blofield, Lingwood, Beighton, Cantley, Reedham, Freethorpe and Halvergate all played in this league. Obviously the pitches weren't very good in those days, so if any of the teams scored 50 runs they were doing very well.

My first memories of watching Halvergate play were in the early 1950s when they were playing on the late Club President's Halvergate Lawn - namely Mr. Myrus Sutton. In those days the club played in the old local George Beck League with other teams such as Freethorpe, Runham, Stokesby, Fleggburgh, Filby, Ormesby, Martham, Hemsby and Caister. I remember seeing one of the club's stalwarts from that era, the late Clem Mallett score 108 on the Lawn against Filby. I was to take over as Club Secretary from Clem when he stepped down from office after many years. I went on to hold the job from 1965 until 2009, when I had to stand down because of health problems. The role was then taken over by Steve Utting who does a first class job to this day. The highlight of the Club's time in the George Beck League, was winning the Loveday Cup Final once during the 1950s, and again in the early 1960's when we beat a strong Caister team to take the Cup. The final used to be played on the Seacroft Holiday Camp ground on August Bank Holiday Monday. Many people from the Village would come along to support the Club and enjoy a day out.

Another highlight during that era was winning the Norfolk Junior Cup at the Old Lakenham Cricket ground when we beat Whissonsett in the Final. Two other appearances in the final unfortunately weren't so memorable - losing twice to local rivals, Acle.

In the meantime the George Beck League folded and the Club had to play friendly matches for a time. At this time, the Club also lost the use of The Lawn as their home ground and were forced to play their home matches at the Beaconsfield Recreation Ground in Gt. Yarmouth. During this time the club reached the final of the 20/20 Coronation Cup Final three times losing twice before finally winning in 1969 under David Hannant's Captaincy when we beat local rivals Acle in the final. Unfortunately, I was unable to witness this great win due to an enforced hospital stay.

The Club joined the Norfolk League in 1975 when there were only three divisions, and quickly gained promotion to the first division. In 1980 we had to leave the Beaconsfield Ground but luckily were offered the use of the British Sugar Ground in Cantley.

Finally, in 1983, we were able to move back to Halvergate when the new Village Playing Field was opened on a lovely summer's day in June. After many years of hard work and fund raising by the Playing Field Committee, Mr Ben Beck declared the playing field open on what he described as a momentous day for the Village and a dream come true for him. Halvergate finally had its own Playing Field. The day was marked by an all day cricket match between a present-day team and a past players team captained by Bobby Howard.

Our club grew and strengthened and we were able to form an 'A' team who firstly played friendly games before joining the Norfolk League 'A' Division. In 2000 the Club was fielding two Saturday teams and a Sunday side with the first X1 playing Norfolk Alliance Cricket for a time but sadly with the loss of a number of Players, Halvergate withdrew from the Sunday League and finally in 2012

Top: Winners of the 20/20 Coronation Cup. Back row from left: Mike Key, Richard Croft, Rodney Howard, David Hannant, Jimmy Forder, Brian Brister, Eric Peek, Terry Peek. Front row: Derek Bloomfield, Stewart Mallett, Richard Westgate. Bottom: Edwin receiving the Duck Cup back from Ena Mallett in 2011.

97

dropped their first team from the Alliance and the remaining team found itself playing Norfolk League Division 6.

However, to my relief the Club has rallied round thanks to the efforts of Club Secretary Steve Utting and his Committee and we Cricket Fans have just spent an enjoyable Summer of Cricket at the Playing Field and away grounds watching some outstanding performances. Young Luke Hannant topped the batting averages and golden oldie Graham Harrop topped the bowling averages with notable performances from many of the other players.

The Club now boasts an under 14 team and runs coaching sessions for the youngsters which hopefully will be the future of the Club.

I am proud to have always been involved with a Village Club like Halvergate who have a great spirit amongst its Committee, Players and supporters. From those who prepare the wicket and outfield, to the superb tea ladies and the Playing Field Committee who provide such first class facilities.

Such Happy Memories.

**1952 Cricket Team**

# WAR MEMORIAL.

This is located on the Green at the junction of The Street and the Sandhole on the west side of the street. Three sides commemorate the WWI villagers.

The words on the memorial are: 'This monument is erected in grateful memory of the men of Halvergate and Tunstall who laid down their lives in H.M. forces in the Great War 1914 – 1918 Their name liveth for evermore".

George Bloom, Frederick Bradshaw, James Beck, Edward Diboll, Evelyn Everson, Valentine Foster,  Hiram Call, William Hunn, Stephen Hewitt, Herbert Knights, Albert Mallett, Clement Mallett, Ambrose Newson, Wilfred Smith, Charles Springall, James Springall, Albert Watts, Edward Youngs.

On the forth side is commemorated from the 1939 1945 War:
Herbert Barrett, Jack Fransham, and Eric Jermy.

**Above: The War Memorial, photograph supplied by Joy Brock.**

**Right: Rita Stone by the War memorial in the 1950s. Supplied by Christine Sparrow.**

## RODNEY HOWARD REMEMBERS:

I was born down The City in Halvergate on 4/8/1935; my mother was Gertie Springall from Farm House, Tunstall Road. She was born on 20/12/1904. My Dad was Albert Howard born in Reedham, on 22/7/1903. Brought up in Freethorpe, he

From top left: Harry Springall, Henry Springall, Amelia Springall, Charles Springall, John Gravenor, Mary Ann Gravenor, Jack Springall and Gertie Springall at the farmhouse on Tunstall Road circa 1910. Photograph supplied by Rodney Howard.

met mum and they were married at Halvergate Methodist Chapel on 10/6/1930. They had 2 boys and 2 girls. Irene born 18/ 11/1931, died 23 /2/ 1933. Dennis born 4/I0/1933, he died in 2009, one year after his wife Jean died. Me (Rodney), born 4/8/1935. Gwen born 9/2/1938, she married Cecil Mallet at Halvergate Church in 1960.

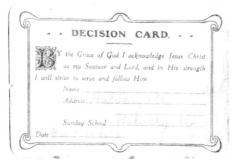

Halvergate was a wonderful village to be brought up in. Sport was and still is well looked after. I played my football and cricket for the village teams, and retired as cricket chairman at the age of 65.

The City, Halvergate, as I remember:
The top left house belonged to the Knights family, top right was Mr Waters.

100

Below the Knights garden the first cottage was Boyse and the second cottage the Malletts.

On the other side was 3 cottages, the first had a large pear-tree. After these there was another cottage occupied by "Bunch" Carter, then after him Wilfred Lake and then Charlie Carter.

Opposite cottage 1 was Mrs Johnson and then Mr & Mrs Audrey. (She was a Ladies Hairdresser)

Around the Loke was Mr & Mrs Dick Taylor then Mrs Taylor's parents Mr & Mrs Mallet.

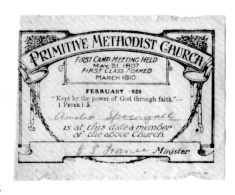

Back in The City, Fred Lake and family who lived opposite, had farm buildings behind our house, had cowsheds and milked twice a day, this was by hand as they had no machines then.

Rodney, Gwen & Dennis Howard

Cottages at the bottom on left first the Rushbrook family, with the Carters as their neighbours Opposite side of the road another family, then behind them the last family down the City were the Chummeys. In front of them was the well where we had to take our bucket to get drinking water, pretty close to 100 yards.

From 5 years of age we attended Halvergate Primary School, by our eleventh birthday we took exams for Higher school or attend Freethorpe School which was my route of education in those days, there were no coaches or buses to get you to school. We were issued with bicycles, which our parents had to keep in top condition.

At 15 I worked for Myrus Sutton on Mack's Farm just into Freethorpe at the end of Halvergate Road. In 1954 we lived at a council house number 12 Mill Road, Halvergate. The rent at that time was 9/3d per week and the rates were 12/7d.

At 18 I was called up for National Service, I requested Royal Air Force and was eventually successful.

In 1965, I left the village and I got married to a Norwich girl, Jill Andrea Votier and we went to live in Drayton.

# GERALD J. MALLETT REMEMBERS

Now aged 87 I have lived in Halvergate all my life. I left school at 14 years and started work on R.J. More's Farm at Tunstall. About thirty plus men worked there, and about the same number of horses, drilling, ploughing, harvesting, hay-making, muck carting, cattle feeding etc.

I now live at Hill-View on Mill Road near the old mill and have been here for 58 years. This mill was a corn mill and the miller was Mr Wright. He ground the corn for flour and made bread as there was a bakery alongside the mill.

I remember when I was about 8 to 10 years old we had a very bad winter: roads were blocked and snow drifts 6 to 10 feet high.

Gerald Mallett & John Willimott in Egypt

At More's Farm I fattened cattle in sheds when I was aged 15 and 16. For those 2 years there was 40 head of cattle. Mr More was also a fruit farmer growing blackcurrants. When the fruit was ready for gathering I was one who weighed the fruit and then brought them to the farm to be loaded onto lorries to be taken away to make jam or blackcurrant drink.

There was a blacksmith building in the village and I have taken as many as three horses tied together to have new shoes fitted.

At 18 I received my papers to enlist in the army during WWII. I reported to Brittania Barracks which is now the prison and did 16 weeks training, came home on embarkation leave for 14 days, and back I went knowing I was going to the front line. Within weeks of returning I was in the front line infantry and crossed the Rhine and the Elbe. I can only describe this as 'like Hell let loose', believe me. I think to this day 'How the Hell did I survive?' lots of my comrades didn't.

After the war I returned to More's Farm when tractors and machinery took the place of horses so labour had to be reduced. I worked at Pettits of Reedham for a while collecting foul, game rabbit to be killed. Later I left and went self-employed, beet hoeing, lifting beet and reed cutting around the Broads and various other jobs. I had the newspaper business in Halvergate for twenty one years. I retired at 65 years old but did a few odd jobs in the village and I am still going. Sadly I have now lost my dear wife Myrtle after 58 years of married life. I miss her big time, and life will never be the same.

102

## BRENDA PAWSEY (NEE SAUNDERS) REMEMBERS

One of my earliest childhood memories is that of standing outside Halvergate School gates waving a Union Jack flag as the royal cars drove past during Queen Elizabeth and Prince Philip's trip to Norfolk following the coronation in 1953. all the school children received a New Testament Bible and a commemorative coronation mug. I often wanted to sip my nightly bedtime Ovaltine from that special mug but was not allowed to as it was placed high on the dresser for display only. (I still have them all: the cloth flags are still waved on Royal occasions!)

Following my mother's death in London I was brought as a baby to live in Halvergate by my aunt and uncle, Emma and Reginald Waters, who were also my godparents. We lived at Halvergate House and then moved into Rose Cottage on Tunstall Road (now known as White Acres). Reg was a stockman for Robert J. More and I spent many times with him in the bullock yard while he fed them with skeps of wet steaming pulp collected from Cantley Factory. Some of his cattle won prizes at the Royal Norfolk Shows. He had a cart horse called Molly and a tumbrel into which he collected mangolds from the fields in all weathers. During the winter months his hands always got chapped and cracked and he had a tin of Snowfire that he warmed by the fire and rubbed into his fingers.

I attended the Halvergate School and was taught by Mrs Barbara Forster and Mrs Allum who was the head mistress. I enjoyed school dinners cooked by Mrs Vickers but I dreaded the lukewarm 1/3rd of a pint of daily milk. This was delivered free for every child and placed in a crate in the fireplace to warm before playtime. Thinking back we received an excellent all round education with great emphasis on spelling, grammar, handwriting, poetry, prose and 'times-tables'.

Tea-time at home was often taken in the twilight with the light and warmth of the farmhouse fire, toast using a long handled toasting fork and homemade jam. Sundays were set aside for Church or Chapel: we attended Church but I always wanted to be a 'Chapel girl' at Anniversary time when all the girls were beautifully dressed in new 'rig-outs' and said their pieces on the platform. The Church Sunday school was run by Mrs Waters and Mrs Dack, and many attended from Moulton. Every year there was a nativity play at Christmas. A ladies sewing circle was held in the Vicarage to which I walked to after school and learnt knitting, embroidery, and sewing skills. They made socks and gloves on four needles, tea cosies, aprons, chair backs and antimacassars, all manner of household articles, doll's and children's clothes to be sold at the summer fete and Christmas sales in the Church Hall.

My love of music was encouraged and I was taught to play the piano and the Halvergate church organ. Piano lessons cost us 5 shillings and organ lessons 10 shillings, quite an outlay from a farm-workers wages each week, so the church contributed half the cost in return for playing at their Sunday Services. I've been a church organist in these parishes ever since.

Every summer we picked blackcurrants at the Knoll and Crammer in Tunstall on More's farm to earn a shilling or two. The lorry would collect pickers from the surrounding villages and this was an extra source of much needed income. The money we earned in summer holidays helped pay for my school uniform when I went to the Great Yarmouth High School for girls. Many women also went 'Big Budding' which was on fruit bushes and potato picking in the fields.

In 1958 I won a national Brooke Bond Tea competition when I entered an article on the Australian Koala bear in my best handwriting. The prize was a trip to Australia – I never went. What a missed opportunity, but travel was not so common in those days, especially to the other side of the world. We were soon to move to Wickhampton so mum thought it would be a good idea to ask for a new bicycle instead. A representative from the company visited the school for the presentation along with a hamper of delicious luxury Australian foods. From then I cycled to and from school, even using it in later years to transport my daughters Emma- Kate and Hannah -Jane in a seat on the back when it was their turn to attend Halvergate School. I still have the bicycle to this day – rather rusty and dilapidated – now used as a garden feature with hanging baskets and plant pots. How's that for recycling?

## TUNSTALL DYKE & STAITHE

**Tunstall Dyke** is about 0.8 mile long and runs in a WSW direction from the south side of the River Bure at about TG432095 passing under the Acle New Road and the Acle –Yarmouth railway. It was at one time navigable and at the end of the dike is **Tunstall Staithe**, where the Powley family once lived in a wooden building and kept a trading wherry. The family were also coal dealers bringing coal up the Bure, and down the Tunstall Dyke. Prior to the introduction of the motor lorry this was perhaps the simplest method of transporting heavy loads of coal and other heavy goods into the Tunstall village from Great Yarmouth or Norwich as there was only one track into the village.

The last wherry to navigate the dyke is reported to have been 'The Albert and Alexandra' in about 1897. This was an 18 ton wherry owned by Joseph Powley. When unloaded it was difficult to get the vessel under the New Road hump-back Tunstall Bridge and under the railway bridge. It was also difficult to negotiate the bridges when fully laden when the water level was low.
The Powley family had previously owned a wherry called 'Tunstall Trader' and a 14 ton wherry called 'The Maid'.

Joseph Powley was listed in the census returns of 1841 through to 1891, when he died age 82, as a boatman, wherry owner and coal-merchant. Other members of the family, his sons William and John, were also listed as boatmen.

## ELECTRICITY
This arrived in the villages in about 1928. The isolated properties on the marshes, however, remained without mains electricity. Some now have their own generators.

## MAINS WATER
Wells were common throughout until mains water came to the villages in 1960. Some properties, especially those across the marshes, also collected water in large cisterns from the building roof.

## SEWERAGE
Properties had cesspits till mains sewers were built in the 1970s.

## GAS
Mains gas has not been brought into the villages.

## STREET LIGHTING
There is no electric street lighting in the villages.

## TELEPHONE
Some private telephones arrived in Halvergate in the late 1920s.
The public telephone kiosk was installed later on The Street. It is a type K6 kiosk designed by Giles Gilbert Scott in 1935. It is now a Grade II listed building.

## DOCTORS
The earliest mention of a doctor in the village was in the 1937 directory which list Cyril Fletcher as a surgeon.

## POLICE
The first mention of a constable in Halvergate was Herbert Woodgate in the 1916 directory. A police house was built on the east side of the Street and in the 1940s it was occupied by constable Race.

Above: William and Pamela Gossling (nee Waters) at Bakers Road. He was the Overseer, Rate Collector and Clerk to Halvergate and Tunstall Parishes. Below: 1950s view of Bakers Road. Photographs from Joy Brock

**OCCUPATIONS:**

This list shows the number of each occupation listed in the 1861 & 1891census returns for both Halvergate and Tunstall. No distinction is made here regarding whether the people are employers or employees. In some cases, such as for example domestic servant, parlour maid, and housemaid, they have been grouped together for simplification. Some people were listed with more than one job, for example George Lincoln in 1861 was listed as both innkeeper and shepherd, so he and others with more than one occupation, is represented twice in the table.

The figures clearly show that most people were employed in farming, agriculture and related jobs, and many more were employed in domestic service.

| Listed Occupation | Halvergate 1861 | Tunstall 1861 | Halvergate 1891 | Tunstall 1891 |
|---|---|---|---|---|
| Agricultural Carter | 2 | | | |
| Agricultural/farm Lab | 109 | 27 | 62 | 21 |
| Bailiff | 3 | 1 | | |
| Basket Maker | | | 1 | |
| Blacksmith | 7 | | 4 | |
| Boatman /wherryman | | 2 | | 1 |
| Bricklayer | 5 | | 8 | |
| Brickmaker | 1 | | | |
| Butcher | 2 | | 2 | |
| Carpenter | 6 | 1 | 3 | |
| Carrier | 1 | | | |
| Cook | | | 4 | 1 |
| Coachman | | | 1 | |
| Corn miller | 2 | | 2 | |
| Cowkeeper | | | 1 | |
| Dairymaid | 3 | | 1 | |
| Draper Assistant | | | 1 | |
| Dressmaker/tailoress | 5 | 1 | 4 | 1 |
| Errand boy | | | | 1 |
| Farmer | 6 | 1 | 2 | 3+3sons |
| Fisherman | | 2 | 2 | |
| Gardener | 1 | | 4 | |
| Gentleman | 1 | | | |
| Gamekeeper | 1 | | | 1 |
| General labourer | | | 9 | |
| Governess | | | 2 | |
| Grocer | 7 | | 3 | |
| Groom | 4 | | 4 | |
| Hay Dealer | | | 2 | |
| Herring Seller | 1 | | | |
| Horse leader | | 1 | | |
| House keeper | 13 | 1 | 4 | |
| Housemaid/Dom Servant | 12 | 2 | 13 | 3 |
| Innkeeper/Publican | 3 | 1 | 2 | 1 |
| Laundress | | | 4 | |
| Marketman / Mkt Gardener | 1 | | 1 | |

| | | | | |
|---|---|---|---|---|
| Marsh man | 5 | 2 | 10 | 6 |
| Nurse | 1 | | 1 | |
| Nurse maid | 1 | | 1 | |
| Parish Clerk | 1 | | | |
| Pig dealer | 1 | | 1 | |
| Plumber / glazier | 1 | | 1 | |
| School teachers | 3 | | 3 | |
| Sheppard | 2 | | 1 | 1 |
| Shoe binder | 2 | | | |
| Boot/Shoemaker/cordwainer | 5 | | 4 | |
| Steam Engine Proprietor | | | 1 | |
| Steam Engine Driver | | | 1 | |
| Thatcher | 1 | | 1 | |
| Tollgate Keeper | | 1 | | |
| Veterinary Surgeon | 2 | | 2 | |
| Vicar | 1 | | 1 | |
| Washerwoman | 2 | | | |
| Watchmaker | | | | 1 |
| Wheelwright | | | 3 | |
| Workwoman | 4 | | | |

## TUNSTALL SURNAMES from Census Returns.

| SURNAME | 1841 | 1851 | 1861 | 1871 | 1881 | 1891 | 1901 | 1911 |
|---|---|---|---|---|---|---|---|---|
| ALLEN | | | | | | | | 5 |
| AMIS | 1 | | | | | | | |
| ARNUP | | 10 | 7 | 10 | 10 | 10 | 4 | 2 |
| ASHBY | | | 3 | | | | | |
| BARBER | | | | | 6 | 2 | 1 | 1 |
| BATES | | | | | | 4 | | |
| BAUER? | | | 4 | | | | | |
| BECK | 7 | | 6 | 4 | 8 | 13 | 15 | |
| BLAND | | | | | 2 | | | |
| BOULT | 5 | | | | | | | |
| BOWMAN | 1 | | | | | | | |
| BREEZE | | | | | | 1 | | |
| BRINDED | | | | | | 3 | | |
| BROWN | | | | | | | 5 | |
| BULLARD | | | | 4 | | | | |
| BURGES | | | 1 | | | | | |
| BUSSEY | 1 | | | | | | | |
| CAR | | 1 | | | | | | |
| CARTER | | | | | | | 8 | 8 |
| CLARE | | | | | | | | 1 |
| CLARK(E) | 2 | 1 | | | | | | |
| COOK | | | | 1 | | | | |
| COX | | | | 4 | | | | |
| CRICKMORE | | | | | | | | 9 |
| CURTIS | | 8 | 4 | | | | | |
| DANN | | | 1 | | | | | |
| DAY | | | | | | | | 1 |

| | | | | | | | | |
|---|---|---|---|---|---|---|---|---|
| DIVER | 4 | 1 | | | | | | |
| DURRANT | 1 | 1 | | | | | | |
| ELLIS | | | | | | 4 | | |
| EVERSON | | 2 | | | | | | |
| FIDDY | | | | 1 | | | | |
| FIELD | | | 1 | | | | | |
| FLINT | | | | | | | | 0 |
| FRANCIS | 3 | 4 | | | | | | |
| FRANSHAM | 4 | 9 | 10 | 11 | 9 | 8 | 6 | 4 |
| GIDNEY | | 1 | | | | | | |
| GILBERT | 1 | | | | | | | |
| GILLETT | | 4 | | | 2 | | | |
| GOFF | | | | | | 1 | | |
| GOLDER? | | | | | 9 | | | |
| GOOCH | | | | 1 | | | | |
| GREEN | | 1 | | | | | | |
| GUNTON | | | | | 6 | | | |
| HARPER | | | 4 | | | 5 | 8 | 5 |
| HARRISON | | | 2 | | | | | |
| HEWITT | | | | | | 1 | | |
| HOLLIS | 2 | | | | | | | |
| HOLMES | | 2 | 2 | | | | | |
| HOWARD | | | | 1 | | | | |
| HOWELL | | 6 | 4 | | | | | |
| HOWLET | | 1 | | | | | | |
| JARMYN | 2 | | | | | | | |
| JOHNSON | | | | | | | | 2 |
| JONES | 5 | 9 | 3 | 4 | | 1 | | 5 |
| KEY | | | | | | | 2 | 2 |
| LAKE | | | 2 | | | | | |
| LAWN | | 9 | | 3 | 3 | 2 | 1 | |
| LIDDLE | | 5 | 5 | | | | | |
| LINFORD | | | | | | | 1 | |
| LUBBOCK | | | | | | | 3 | |
| MALLETT | 1 | | | | | 11 | 9 | 12 |
| MARSHAL | 1 | 3 | 2 | | | | | |
| MINISTER | 1 | | | 3 | | | | |
| MITCHELL? | | | | 1 | | | | |
| MORE | | | | | 1 | 5 | 3 | 0 |
| MORSE | 2 | | | | | | | |
| MOSS | 10 | 4 | | | 1 | | 1 | |
| MYHILL | | | 1 | | | | | |
| NEWSON | | | | | | | | 3 |
| NICHOLLS | | | | 7 | 5 | 6 | 6 | |
| OLIVER | | | | | | | | 2 |
| PALMER | 2 | | | | | | | 1 |
| PARFITT | | | | | | | 7 | |
| POWLEY | 8 | 9 | 7 | 4 | 6 | 2 | | |
| PRIME | | | | | | | | 1 |
| PULFORD | | 1 | | | | | | |
| RAVEN | 10 | 8 | | | | | | |
| RAYNER | | | | | | 3 | | |

| SURNAME | 1841 | 1851 | 1861 | 1871 | 1881 | 1891 | 1901 | 1911 |
|---|---|---|---|---|---|---|---|---|
| READ | | | | | | 4 | 5 | 6 |
| ROWLAND | | | | | | | | 1 |
| RUMBOLD | | | | | 5 | 4 | | |
| RUSHBROOK | | | | | 4 | | | |
| SHARMAN | 2 | | | | 3 | | | |
| SHEARING | 1 | | | | | | | |
| SKINNER | | 4 | 9 | 8 | 3 | | | |
| SMITH | 14 | 13 | 5 | 4 | | | | |
| SNELLING | | | | | | 2 | | |
| SPRINGALL | | | | | | | | |
| STACEY | | | | 1 | | | | |
| STERLING | | 1 | | | | | | |
| SWASH | 1 | | | | | | | |
| TOOLEY | | | | | | | | 2 |
| TOVELL | | | | | | 7 | 8 | 5 |
| TURNER | | | 4 | 3 | 4 | | | |
| WARD | 1 | 5 | 3 | 9 | 1 | | | |
| WATERS | | | | | | 9 | 11 | 6 |
| WATSON | | 1 | | | | | | |
| WATTS | 15 | 11 | 15 | 13 | 2 | 2 | | |
| WILKNS | | | 4 | | | | | |
| WILLIMONT | | 1 | | | | | | |
| WOOLNOUGH | | 1 | | | | | | |
| WYMER | | | | | | 6 | 12 | |
| YOUNGS | | | | | 9 | 11 | 12 | 5 |

**HALVERGATE** Surnames from census returns

| SURNAME | 1841 | 1851 | 1861 | 1871 | 1881 | 1891 | 1901 | 1911 |
|---|---|---|---|---|---|---|---|---|
| ADAMS | | | | | 2 | 2 | | |
| AGUS | | 1 | | | | | | |
| AMIS | | 1 | | 1 | | | | |
| ALDEN | | | 1 | | | | | |
| ALEXANDER | | | | | | | | 1 |
| ALLARD | | | | | 1 | | | |
| ANDREWS | 5 | 6 | 9 | 3 | 3 | | | |
| ARNUP | | | | | | 1 | 5 | 1 |
| AUSTIN | | | | | | 2 | | |
| BAKER | 1 | | | | | | | |
| BANHAM | | | | 5 | 5 | 4 | 5 | 4 |
| BARBER | | | | | | 6 | 10 | 9 |
| BATLEY | | | | 1 | | | | |
| AVERSON(?) | | 5 | | | | | | |
| BANE | | 1 | | | | | | |
| BALDERSON | | 1 | | | | | | |
| BARNES | | 1 | | | | | | |
| BETMAN(?) | | 1 | | | | | | |
| BARNARD | | | | | | | | 1 |
| BEAN | | | | | | 1 | | |
| BECK | 10 | 26 | 17 | 11 | 14 | 1 | 7 | 11 |
| BELL | | | | | | 1 | | |
| BELSTEAD(?) | | 2 | | | | | | |

| | | | | | | | | |
|---|---|---|---|---|---|---|---|---|
| BELSON | 4 | | | | | | | |
| BETTS | | | | | 4 | 9 | | |
| BEVERLEY | 1 | 1 | | | | | | |
| BIRD | 1 | | | | | | | |
| BLAND | | 1 | 7 | | | | | |
| BLOOM | | | | | | | 8 | 4 |
| BLYTH(E) | | | 2 | 1 | 1 | | | |
| BOON | | 1 | | | | 1 | | |
| BOULT | | | | | 7 | | | |
| BOWMAN | | | | 1 | | | | |
| BRADSHAW | | | | | | 3 | 10 | 11 |
| BRETT | | | 1 | | | | | |
| BRISTER | | | | | | - | 5 | 9 |
| BRINDED | | | | | 1 | 5 | | |
| BROOKS | 2 | 4 | | | | | | |
| BROWN(E) | 15 | 19 | 10 | 12 | 10 | 7 | 11 | 15 |
| BURGES | 1 | | | | | | | |
| BURNE | | | 1 | | | | | |
| BURRELL | | | | | | | 1 | |
| BUSH | 5 | | | | | | | 1 |
| CALLOW | 2 | 2 | 1 | | | | | |
| CALVER | | | | | | | | 1 |
| CACTON(?) | | 2 | | | | | | |
| CAN | | | | | | | | 1 |
| CARTER | 1 | 1 | 25 | 25 | 32 | 41 | 33 | 36 |
| CASTER? | | | | | | | | 4 |
| CHANEY | 3 | | | | | | | |
| CHAPMAN | | | 1 | | 2 | | | |
| CHARLISH? | | | | | | 1 | | |
| CHESTER | 2 | | | | | | | |
| CHURCH | | 2 | 1 | | | | | |
| CLARK(E) | | 1 | 1 | 3 | | | | |
| COCKERILL | 6 | | | 4 | 4 | 2 | 2 | 2 |
| COLLINS | 1 | | | | | | | |
| COX | 2 | 2 | 2 | | | | | |
| CRANE | | | 2 | 4 | 3 | 5 | | |
| CREMER | | | | | 1 | | | |
| CRISP | | 1 | | | | | | |
| CULLUM | | | 1 | 1 | | | | |
| CUTTING | | | | | 1 | | | |
| DALLIMORE | | | | | | 7 | 4 | 4 |
| DANIELS | | | 3 | | | | | |
| DAWDY | 4 | 3 | | | | | | |
| DAWSON | 1 | | | 2 | 1 | | | 4 |
| DARNELL | | | | 1 | | | | |
| DIBOLL | | | | | | | 3 | 2 |
| ENGLAND | | 2 | | | | | | |
| DINGLE | | | | | 1 | | 2 | 2 |
| DIVERS | 1 | | 1 | | | | | |
| DOVE | | | | | 1 | | | |
| DRAKE | | | | | | 1 | 1 | |
| EASTAUGH | 1 | | | | | | | |

| Name | | | | | | | | |
|---|---|---|---|---|---|---|---|---|
| EASTER | | | | 1 | | | | |
| EATON | | | | 1 | | | | |
| ECCLESTONE | 1 | | | | | | | |
| EDWARDS | | | | | | | | 5 |
| EMMON(D?) | 4 | | | | 1 | | | |
| EMMS | | | | 2 | | | | |
| ETHERIDGE | | | | | 4 | | | |
| EVERSON | 21 | 27 | 24 | 5 | 9 | 10 | 8 | 6 |
| FAKE | | | | | 1 | | | |
| FARMAN | 4 | 3 | 3 | | | | | |
| FARROW | | | | | 1 | | | |
| FEEK | | | | | 1 | | | |
| FITT | 1 | | | | | | | |
| FLINT | 4 | 7 | 12 | 8 | 8 | 12 | 20 | 17 |
| FORD | | 1 | | | | | | |
| FORDER | | | | | 2 | 2 | 2 | 1 |
| FORSTER | | | | | | | | 2 |
| FOULGER | | | | | | | 1 | 1 |
| FOX | | | | | 1 | | | |
| FRANCIS | 6 | 6 | | | | | | |
| FRANSHAM | 10 | 2 | 11 | 11 | 11 | 4 | 12 | 10 |
| FRETT | | 2 | | | 1 | | | |
| FROST | | | | | | | | 1 |
| GARWOOD | | | | 2 | 4 | 7 | 4 | 2 |
| GAZE | | | | | 4 | 9 | 8 | |
| GEARY | | | | | | 1 | | |
| GEDGE | | | 2 | 2 | 2 | 2 | 2 | 2 |
| GIBBS | 1 | | | | | | | |
| GILLEN? | 1 | 1 | | | | | | |
| GILBERT | 4 | 1 | | | 5 | 5 | 2 | 2 |
| GILLET(T) | 17 | 10 | 11 | 5 | 4 | 11 | 8 | 6 |
| GOFFIN | | | | | 1 | | | |
| GOLDSPINK | | | | | | 1 | | |
| GOOCH | 10 | 8 | 2 | | 1 | 1 | 1 | 1 |
| GOODCHILD | | | | | | 1 | | |
| GOSLING | | 7 | 5 | 15 | 6 | 4 | 4 | 3 |
| GOWER | | | 1 | | | | | |
| GOWING | | | | 1 | | | | |
| GRANT | | | | | | 1 | | |
| GRAVENER | 1 | 6 | 6 | 3 | 3 | 2 | 2 | 2 |
| GREEN | 1 | 1 | 6 | | | | | |
| GRINT | | | | | | | | 3 |
| GRAY | | 1 | | | | | | |
| GRIMBLE | | 1 | | | | | | |
| HALCON | | | 1 | | | | | |
| HALESWORTH | | 8 | 4 | 4 | 2 | | | |
| HANTON | | | 1 | | | | | |
| HART | | | 1 | | | | | |
| HARPER | 12 | 12 | 13 | 21 | 22 | 20 | 19 | 22 |
| HUBBARD | | 1 | | | | | | |
| HEBDITCH | | | | | | - | | 1 |
| HEWITT | | 2 | 1 | 8 | 9 | 9 | | 10 |

112

| | | | | | | | | |
|---|---|---|---|---|---|---|---|---|
| IVES | 9 | | | | | | | |
| HIGH | 1 | | | | | 1 | 5 | 9 |
| HILTON | | | | | 1 | | | |
| HINDES | 5 | | | | | | | |
| HOLSEY | 8 | | | | | | | |
| HOLT | 1 | | | | | | | |
| HOOK | | | 7 | | | | | |
| HOWARD | 8 | 3 | 3 | 3 | 8 | 1 | 1 | 8 |
| HUNN | | | | | | | 7 | 12 |
| HUNT | | | | | | 1 | | |
| HUNTING | | 4 | 8 | 4 | 6 | 3 | 1 | |
| HURST | | | | 2 | | | | |
| IVES | 9 | 6 | 9 | | | | | |
| JACOBS | 2 | 1 | 1 | 2 | | | | |
| JENNIS | | | | | | 1 | | |
| JERMY | | | | | | | 1 | 5 |
| JOHNSON | | | | | | | | 2 |
| JONES | 30 | 27 | 33 | 20 | 25 | 33 | 23 | 11 |
| JOYCE | | | | | 1 | | | |
| KEABLE | | | | | | 3 | | |
| KELNER | 1 | | | | | | | |
| KETTLE | 2 | 5 | 2 | 2 | 2 | 1 | | |
| KEYS(?) | | | | | 1 | | | |
| KIDNER | | | | | | | 4 | 3 |
| KING | | | | | 1 | | | |
| KIRK | 3 | 4 | 7 | 5 | 2 | 1 | | |
| KNIGHTS | | | | | 1 | 6 | 5 | 7 |
| LACON | | | | 2 | | | | |
| LAKE | | | | 3 | | - | | 13? |
| LANDALL? | | | | | 1 | | | |
| LAWN | 14 | 7 | 3 | | 1 | - | | 1 |
| LEMAN | | | 1 | | | | | |
| LINCOLN | 5 | 4 | 10 | 4 | | | | |
| LOVELL | | | | | 5 | 1 | | |
| LUBBOCK | | | | | | 1 | | |
| MACK | | | | 3 | | | | |
| MAYES | | | | | | 2 | | |
| MALANY? | | | | | | | | 1 |
| MALLETT | 40 | 39 | 35 | 41 | 51 | 48 | 42 | 55 |
| MANN | | | | | | | | 1 |
| MARRIOTT | | | | | | | | 2 |
| MARSHALL | | 2 | 1 | | | | | |
| MEAL | | | | 1 | | | | |
| MESSENGER | 1 | 1 | | | | | | |
| MINGAY | | 3 | 1 | | | | | |
| MINISTER | 8 | 8 | 6 | 3 | 3 | | | |
| MOLL | | | 5 | | | | | |
| MORE | | | | | | | | 5 |
| MORSE | 2 | | 8 | | | | | |
| MOSS | | 9 | 3 | 11 | 2 | | | |
| MOUNTSEER? | | | | | 1 | | | |
| MURRELL | | | 1 | | | | | |

113

| | | | | | | | | |
|---|---|---|---|---|---|---|---|---|
| MUTTON | 4 | 8 | 10 | 15 | 16 | 23 | 11 | 9 |
| NASH | | | | 1 | | | | |
| NEAL | 1 | | | | | | | |
| NEWSON | | 1 | 1 | 1 | | - | 7 | 6 |
| NICHOLLS | 14 | 20 | 25 | 17 | 19 | 13 | 21 | 32 |
| NORTON | | | | 2 | | | | |
| NINNIM? | 1 | | | | | | | |
| OMEROD | | | 1 | 1 | 1 | | | |
| OLLEY | | | 6 | 5 | 4 | 5 | 2 | 1 |
| PAGRAM | | 1 | 1 | | | | | |
| PALMER | 3 | | | 1 | | | | |
| PARKER | 2 | | | | | | | |
| PATMAN | 1 | | | | | | | |
| PHILLIPS | | | | | | | 7 | 6 |
| PITCHERS | 6 | 6 | 4 | 6 | | 1 | | 1 |
| POOLEY | | | 1 | 1 | | | | |
| POTTLE | 1 | | | | | | | |
| PULFORD | 1 | | | | | | | |
| PUNCHER | 1 | | | | | | | |
| PURDY | | | | 1 | | | | |
| PYGALL | | | | 1 | | | | |
| QUANTRILL | | | | 1 | | | | |
| RAISBRAY? | | | | | 4 | | | |
| RANN | 2 | | | | | | | |
| RAVEN | 1 | 1 | | | | | | |
| REEVE | | | | | | 1 | | |
| RISEBROOK | | | 11 | | | | | |
| ROGERS | 4 | | | | | | | |
| ROPE | 1 | | | | | | | |
| RUDD(?) | | 1 | | | | | | |
| ROSE | | | | | | | | 4 |
| ROULE | 1 | | | | | | | |
| ROWLAND | 6 | 7 | 7 | 2 | 2 | 10 | 7 | 8 |
| RUMBOLD | 3 | | | | | | | |
| RUSHBROOK | 12 | 16 | | 7 | 6 | 8 | 10 | 4 |
| RUSHMER | 6 | 7 | 2 | 2 | | | | |
| RUSHWOOD? | | | | | 2 | | | |
| RUSSELL | | 1 | 1 | | | | | |
| SADLER | 8 | 11 | | 3 | 5 | 5 | 4 | 4 |
| SAMPSON | | | | | | 1 | | |
| SAINT | | 4 | | | | | | |
| SALES | | | | 1 | | | | |
| SANDELL | | | | 1 | | | | |
| SEARL? | | | 1 | 1 | | | | |
| SHUCKFORD | 2 | | | | | | | |
| SHARMAN | 3 | 1 | 1 | 2 | | | | |
| SHEPPARD | 1 | | | | | 1 | | |
| SHERRINGHAM | | | | | | 1 | | |
| SHORTEN | 6 | 6 | | | | | | |
| SKIPPON(ER?) | 5 | 11 | 15 | 10 | 15 | 6 | 2+1 | 1 |
| SMITH | 9 | 14 | 7 | 10 | 10 | 12 | 9 | 14 |
| SOLOMON | | | 1 | | | | | |

114

| | | | | | | | | |
|---|---|---|---|---|---|---|---|---|
| SPALDING | | | | | 1 | | | |
| SPINKS | | | 2 | | | | | |
| SPRINGALL | 6 | 10 | 9 | 14 | 19 | 15 | 11 | 13 |
| STARLING | | | | | | - | 1 | 1 |
| STEWARD | | | 1 | | | | | |
| STONE | | | | | 1 | 5 | 5 | 3 |
| STOUT | | | 2 | | | | | |
| SUNTON | | | | | | | | 1 |
| SWALE | | | | | | 1 | | |
| SWASH | 1 | | | | | | | |
| TASTER | | | | | | | | 1 |
| THAXTER | | | 4 | | 1 | | | 1 |
| THOMPSON | | | | | 1 | | | |
| THROWER | | 4 | 7 | | | | | |
| TIDMAN | | | | 4 | 5 | 3 | 2 | 1 |
| TOOKE | | | | | 6 | | | |
| TOOLEY | | | | | | 3 | 1 | |
| TOVELL | | | | | | | | 5 |
| TOWER | 3 | | | | | | | |
| TRETT | | | 2 | 2 | | | | |
| TUNGATE | 2 | | | | | | | |
| TURNER | 17 | 15 | 2 | 6 | | | | |
| VINCE | | | 1? | | | | | |
| VINCENT | | | 6 | | | | | |
| WALES | 2 | 2 | | | | | | |
| WANT | | | | | | 1 | | |
| WARD | 5 | 9 | 12 | 6 | 11 | 12 | 3 | 1 |
| WARFORD | | | | | | 1 | | |
| WARNES | 11 | 9 | 4 | 1 | | | | |
| WATERS | 7 | 5 | 10 | 1 | 5 | 2 | 2 | 4 |
| WATTS | 5 | 10 | 9 | 11 | 8 | 18 | 16 | 6 |
| WATSON | | 1 | | | | | | |
| WALL | | 6 | | | | | | |
| WEBB | | | | 3 | 1 | | | |
| WEBSTER | 1 | | | | | | | |
| WEST | | | 1 | | | | | |
| WHINES | | 1 | | 7 | 6 | 3 | | |
| WILKINSON | 1 | | | | | | | |
| WILSON | | | | 1 | | | | |
| WOODCOCK | | | | | | | 3 | 1 |
| WOODHOUSE | | | 1 | | | | | |
| WOODS | | | | | 1 | | | |
| WOOLNER | | | | | | 2 | | |
| WRIGHT | | | | | | | | 4 |
| WYAND | 5 | 12 | 13 | 10 | 8 | 4 | 7 | 6 |
| WYMER | | | | 1 | 1 | | | |
| YALLOP | | | 1 | | | | | |
| YOUMANS? | | | | 1 | | | | |
| YOUNGS | 4 | 5 | 5 | 7 | 11 | 15 | 14 | 13 |
| SAMMON(?) | | 6 | | | | | | |

# 1841 Voters

| Name | Place | Property | Location |
|---|---|---|---|
| Bately Stephen | Martham | Freehold house and land | James Skinner, tenant |
| Boult Thomas | Tunsta | 50l. occupier | Near the church |
| Cross Thomas | Bastwaugh | 50l. occupier | Near the new road |
| Cross George | Armingland | 50l. occupier | Near the new road |
| Everit Isaac | South Creak | Freehold land | Near the new road |
| | | | |
| Godard Erasmus | Lingwood | Freehold land | Near the new road |
| Gillett William | Halvergate | Freehold house | Marsh road |
| Gillett John | Halvergate | Freehold house and land | Marsh road |
| Gillett George | Halvergate | Freehold house and land | Marsh road |
| Morse James | Tunsta | 50l. occupier | Everitt Levell, near Boat dyke |
| Skinner James, junr. | | 50l. occupier | Staithe road |
| | | | |
| Andrew John | Halvergate | Freehold house | marsh road |
| Burges George, Clerk | Norwich | Freehold house and land | Vicarage |
| Boult George | Southtown | Freehold house and land | Edward Dawdy, tenant |
| Bately John | Burlingham St. Andrew | Freehold house and land | Samuel Lawn and Wm. Springall, tenants |
| Bareham Samuel | Southtown, Yarmouth | Freehold land | In Men's level |
| Crow Samuel | Aldeby | Freehold land | James Rushmer, tenant |
| Crow James | Lumpenhoe | Freehold land | Marsh |
| Clarke John | Cantley | Freehold house and land | William Halesworth, tenant |
| Curtis John | Halvergate | Freehold house and land | Wm. Chester and Esther Morse, tenants |
| Dawdy Edward | Narford hall | Land as occupier | Upland and marsh |
| Fountaine Andrew, Esqre. | Markshall | Freehold land | Cyrus Gillett and Richard Gillett, tenants |
| Gillett Cyrus | Halvergate | Freehold house and land | Near the church |
| Gillett William | Halvergate | Freehold house and land | Richard Gillett, tenant |
| Gillett Richard | Halvergate | Freehold house and land | Near Tunstall church |
| Gillett Robert | Halvergate | Farm as occupier | Near the church |
| Howard John | Halvergate | Land as occupier | On the marshes |
| Howard Robert | Halvergate | Freehold land | Near the Sand pit |
| Howard Benjamin | Halvergate | Land as occupier | On the marshes |
| Ives Barzilla | Halvergate | Freehold house and land | In the city |
| Jones Thomas | Halvergate | Freehold house and land | Near the Clay pit |
| Mallett John | Halvergate | Freehold house and land | Near the marshes |
| Mallett James | Yarmouth | Freehold house and land | In the city |
| Nichols Charles | Halvergate | Freehold and copyhold land | William Barber, tenant |
| Palmer Edward | Halvergate | Freehold house and land | James Beck, tenant |
| Rushmer James, senr. | Halvergate | Freehold house and land | Near the church |
| Rushmer James, jr. | Halvergate | Land as occupier | Near the marshes |
| Rushmer Edward | Halvergate | Mill as occupier | Halvergate mill |
| Rope Charles Gillett | Hemblington | Freehold land | Marsh |
| Rumbold Benjamin | Halvergate | Freehold house and land | Near the Clay pit |
| Smith Samuel | Halvergate | Copyhold house and land | Near the church |
| Saut Robert | Halvergate | Freehold house and land | At the Cross ways, city corner |
| Turner Robert | Halvergate | Freehold house and land | In the city |
| Warnes Jacob | Halvergate | Freehold house and land | In the city |
| Wells Thomas | Sco Ruston | Freehold land | Near Sharman's mill |

## Grade II Listed Buildings in Halvergate & Tunstall

| Building | Location |
|---|---|
| Barn 50 Metres N of Halvergate House | Squire's Road. |
| Barn at Hall Farm 30 Metres SSE of War Memorial | The Street. |
| Barn at Hall Farm 61 Metres S-E of War Memorial | Hall Farm Close. |
| Peter and St Paul Church. (Grade I) | The Street |
| Dawdys Farmhouse | The Street. |
| Hall Farm Barn 55 Metres S of War Memorial | . |
| Hall Farm House | Tunstall Road. |
| Halvergate Hall | Hall Farm Close. TG4199806579 |
| Halvergate House and Garden Walls | Squire's Road. TG4198607221 |
| Halvergate Corn Mill | Mill Road. |
| High's Mill | Marshes. |
| K6 Telephone Kiosk | The Street. TG4196906735 |
| Kerrisons Level Drainage Mill | Marshes. |
| Manor House | Tunstall Road. TG4166607921 |
| Mill House and Attached Outbuildings | Mill Road. TG4160505937 |
| Mutton's Mill | Marshes. |
| Red Lion Public House | Marsh Road TG4225806986 |
| Remains of Church of St Peter and St Paul | Low Farm Road. |
| Six Mile House Drainage Mill | Acle New Road. |
| South Walsham Mill | Marshes. |
| Staithe Farm House | Staithe Road. |
| Dawdys Farmhouse | TG4205106723 |
| Stone Cottage | The Street. |
| Stracey Arms Windpump | Acle New Road. |
| The Old Post Office | Old Post Office Court. TG4202306783 |
| The Rookery | Sandhole Road. TG4182106867 |

# THE GILLETT FAMILY.

The Gillett family have been associated with Halvergate and Tunstall for many years. The family is believed to originally come from Gillette, a village in Savoy. One of the descendants of this family, a John Gillett, purchased the Halvergate Estate in 1705. His many descendants spread across Norfolk and beyond but one or two stems of the family remained in Halvergate and Tunstall and carried the Gillett name well into the 20<sup>th</sup> Century.

WILLIAM GILLETT, of Bradfied, in 1563, proved his right to the family arms at the Heralds' Visitation. His descendant, JOHN GILLETT, purchased the Hall estate at Halvergate, co. Norfolk, in 1705. His great-grandson, the late CYRUS GILLETT, Esq. of GILLETTgate Hall, *m.* Sarah, dau. and heiress of Robert Howard, Esq. of Beighton, and dying in 1848, left the following family,

I. ROBERT (present representative of the family), of Halvergate Hall, co. Norfolk, *m.* Harriet, dau. and co-heiress of Robert Howard, Esq.
II. DANIEL, M.A. of Beighton, in holy orders, rector of Geldeston, *m.* Mary-Ann, the other dau. and co-heiress of Robert Howard, Esq.
III. CYRUS, of Postwick Hall, Norfolk.
IV. Edward, M.A. of Shipmeadow, Suffolk, in holy orders. vicar of Runham, Norfolk, *m.* Ellen-Elizabeth, dau. of Capt. George-Edward Francis, of Martham Grange, Norfolk, late of the 77th regt. of foot, and of the East Norfolk militia.
V. Henry, capt. East Kent Militia, *m.* Sarah-Maria, dau. of W.-J. Lysley, Esq., M.P.
VI. Thomas.
I. Sarah.
II. Emma, *m.* Henry Blake, Esq.
III. Louisa, *m.* Rev. George-H. Cooke, M.A., incumbent of St. Matthew's, Thorpe, Norwich.

| Some Gillett family names associated with Halvergate & Tunstall : |
|---|

**1. John Gillett**
sp: Ann
└ 2. John Gillett (b.Abt 1710)
   sp: Mary
   └ 3. John Gillett (b.Abt 1745)
      sp: Lydia Darby
      ├ 4. Cyrus Gillett (b.Abt 1783)
         sp: Sarah Howard (b.Abt 1791)
         └ 5. Robert Gillett (b.Abt 1818)
            sp: Harriet Howard (b.Abt 1820)
            └ 6. Robert Howard Gillett (b.Abt 1844)
               sp: Ellen Doyle (b.Abt 1855)
               └ 7. Cyrus Doyle Gillett (b.Abt 1884)
      └ 4. Richard Gillett (b.Abt 1788)
         sp: Mary (b.Abt 1789)
         └ 5. Caroline A Gillett (b.Abt 1829)
            sp: Robert More
            └ 6. Robert More (b.Abt 1863)

# REFERENCES AND BIBLIOGAPHY.

The Halvergate Chronicles, B. S. Grint, 1984.
The Halvergate Fleet: Past & Present, 0954168305, Sheila Hutchinson 2001.
Freethorpe Past & Present, 9780954168384, Sheila Hutchinson, 2011.
Wickhampton Memories , 9780957462304, Sheila Hutchinson, 2012.
The Lower Bure from Great Yarmouth to Upton, 97809654168360, Sheila Hutchinson, 2008.
Census Returns for Halvergate and Tunstall for 1841, 1851, 1861, 1871, 1881, 1891, 1901 and 1911
Various old Norfolk Directories
Halvergate and Tunstall Tithe Maps and Apportionments
Licence Registers PS8/6/1-4 at Norfolk Records Office.
Websites with useful information include:
www.familysearch.org
www.historic-maps.norfolk.gov.uk
www.old-maps.co.uk

# ACKNOWLEDGEMENTS.

I wish to express my thanks to the following people for supplying information, photographs and contributing to this book.

Charlie Carter, Joy Brock, George Hazell, Desmond Sharman, Gerald Mallett, Rodney Howard, Christine Sparrow, Carol Hannant, Edwin Youngs, John Youngs, Heather Wright, Peter Allard, Ursula Brewer, Brian Grint, Billy Lacey, Brenda Pawsey, Jane Pitchers, the late John Willimott, the late Bertie High, James Black, and Keira Black. Thanks also to the Eastern Daily Press, the Great Yarmouth Mercury, the Norfolk Records Office and the Norwich Library

## Other books by Sheila Hutchinson:

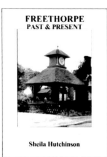

120